To Jared,
Bes "relations"
Graeme + Val

PROPERLY LONG WAY

OUR STORY

8/9/23

VAL WICKS AND GRAEME WICKS

Published in Australia by Sid Harta Books & Print Pty Ltd,
ABN: 34632585293
23 Stirling Crescent, Glen Waverley, Victoria 3150 Australia
Telephone: +61 3 9560 9920, Facsimile: +61 3 9545 1742
E-mail: author@sidharta.com.au

First published in Australia 2022
This edition published 2022
Copyright © Graeme and Val Wicks 2022
Cover design, typesetting: WorkingType (www.workingtype.com.au)

The right of Graeme and Val Wicks to be identified as the Author of the Work has been asserted in accordance with the Copyright, Designs and Patents Act 1988.

All rights reserved. No part of this publication may be reproduced, stored in a retrieval system, or transmitted, in any form or by any means without the prior written permission of the publisher, nor be otherwise circulated in any form of binding or cover other than that in which it is published and without a similar condition being imposed on the subsequent purchaser.

Graeme and Val Wicks
Properly Long Way: Our Story
ISBN: 978-1-922958-04-4 (paperback)
978-0-6456941-7-8 (ebook)
pp330

ABOUT THE AUTHORS

Born in 1949, Val learned to read Enid Blyton's *Secret Seven* and Anna Sewell's *Black Beauty* before she started school. This early aptitude led to a passion for books and a burning desire to write one herself. This is Val's first book but it's 'bones' have been lying around on various bits of paper for a long time. It is the account of her life which spans across three continents and one island as an airways ground hostess, governess, station domestic, manager's wife and bull catcher's sidekick. Val is the mother of three children, 'Ouma' to eight grandchildren and is committed to her Christian faith, following 'The Man' she came to know in the Kimberley forty-eight years ago.

Born in 1951 into a family of seven children at Kingaroy in Queensland, Graeme was an energetic boy with little time for formal education. He left school after completing Grade 10 and headed to the Kimberley to make his own mark on the world. Quickly promoted up the ranks, he eventually managed Mistake Creek and Spring Creek stations before taking on a bull-catching contract for the West Australian government. He has chaired a number of beef industry groups and judged stud and led steer competitions around Queensland, including the Brisbane Exhibition. A committed Christian, he is always ready to lend a hand wherever one is needed.

CONTENTS

Introduction — 1

Part 1

Buenos Aires to Bull Dust — 5

Chapter 1	In the beginning	7
Chapter 2	Growing up	25
Chapter 3	Life beyond school	47
Chapter 4	Off to the 'land Down Under'	65
Chapter 5	Auvergne Station	82
Chapter 6	Auvergne 'pets'	96
Chapter 7	Ellenbrae Station	106
Chapter 8	Nicholson Station	123
Chapter 9	The bush romance	134
Chapter 10	The bush engagement	146
Chapter 11	The Bush wedding at Helen Springs and other stuff	151
Chapter 12	More Helen Springs experiences	167
Chapter 13	Vestey's gypsies	182
Chapter 14	Mistake Creek Station	193

Chapter 15	When the rivers run	207
Chapter 16	Bull catching on the Turner	218
Chapter 17	Back to civilisation	237
Chapter 18	Remarkable reunions	245
Centurion And I Go Riding…		253

Part 2
Trail Rides and Picnic Lunches — 257

Introduction		259
Chapter 1	Manbulloo Station	261
Chapter 2	Off to Spring Creek Station	288
Chapter 3	Nicholson's 'Head Boy'	297
Chapter 4	A stint at Helen Springs	307
Chapter 5	Turbulent times	312
Chapter 6	Love-a-bull Catchers	318

INTRODUCTION

When I reached the Kimberly region in Western Australia in 1972, I was introduced to the endearing way that Aborigines view distance and which forms the overall title of this book. The Aboriginal stockmen we had working for us back then had no formal education and any document they were called upon to sign was accomplished by a cross or thumb print and a written and signatured assurance beside it from the manager, verifying that 'This is Splinter's mark.'

While driving cattle back to camp from a neighbouring station during Graeme's Manbulloo years, the trip seemed to be awfully long and he'd been sitting still much longer than he ever had in his life. Riding around to Larry who was leading the mob, Graeme enquired how much further they had to go. Larry pushed his lips out in the direction they were heading and with an accompanying nod of the head in the same direction as his lips, he said 'Ah, little bit long way.' That obviously meant the few kilometres back to the camp and Graeme would have understood it better when the trip was completed. For extremely long distances, which these men would not have comprehended beyond the reach of their tribal areas, the phrase changed to 'properly long way', and that's what we've settled on for the title of this book. We have both travelled a 'properly long way'.

I have few regrets in my life, but one that stands out most is that I didn't make the time to discover more about my parents and my own roots. Had I known both parents would pass away in their late sixties, I may have felt a greater sense of urgency. Numerous people have expressed similar remorse that they also didn't uncover more of their kin's past.

For this primary reason I determined to write my own story for my children. However, many other acquaintances continue to tell me I should write my story for general consumption. It's difficult for me to understand why really as I've never thought my life would be interesting to anyone else. Nevertheless, I began this task because even though I have kept a diary since the 1980s and earlier, my children are unlikely to wade through them after I've 'moved on'. Trawling through tedious everyday stuff searching for the 'exciting' bits concealed amongst my ramblings over fifty years wouldn't excite me very much either.

My husband Graeme has also been badgered to write a book on numerous occasions so this has become a joint effort containing our lives, apart and together. Two for the price of one!

Introduction

Anything we have written beyond the last ten or fifteen years will be relying largely on a memory that's irrefutably unreliable, a fact discovered when I was reading letters I wrote to my brother in England after he returned them to me for 'posterity'! A few of my very early life experiences are based less on my own fuzzy memory than on my mother's recollections of them.

I would also like to explain that because the Aboriginal dialect was only spoken and never written in our experience, any of the dialect throughout these pages are written as it sounded. There can be no argument as we really don't know the correct spellings.

I have mostly chosen to use first names only except in the case of my own relatives and some friends who are like family to us, mostly because I don't remember half of the surnames and couldn't see the sense in discriminating. Graeme, on the other hand, has included surnames. We both plead ignorance on their spelling also!

I believe every person who has ever lived has a story to tell. How good it would be if everyone wrote their stories to hand down to the next generation, warts and all. Perhaps we wouldn't make so many mistakes and would have ample examples of better (or worse) methods of getting things done.

PART 1

Buenos Aires to Bull Dust

by
Val Wicks

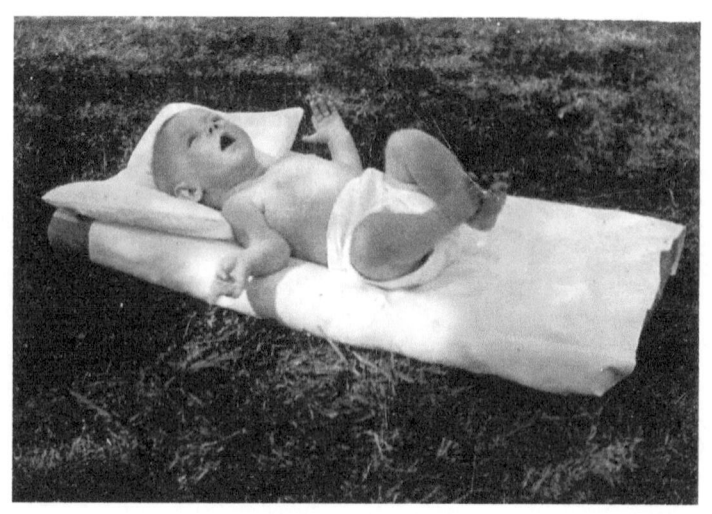

Me as a baby in Argentina

CHAPTER 1

In the beginning

I was born on the 9 October 1949 in Buenos Aires, Argentina, in South America. My father was Gordon Frederick Hames. Somewhere along the line people began calling him Mick, which eventually morphed into Mike. The how's and why's of that name change is one of the many aspects of my dad's life I would love to be able to explain and can't because he couldn't either.

My mother was christened Cecile Josephine Charlesworth. She was always called Jo and I think I can appreciate that since I wouldn't like to be called Cecile very much either.

My father was born in County Cork in Ireland. How long he remained there or where he went to school is unknown but with both his father and mother dead by his eighteenth year, he set sail for Canada where he enrolled in

7

an agricultural college and toured that country by thumbing rides on trains, often illegally I suspect!

My mother on the other hand was born in the Argentine to British parents who had moved to Buenos Aires and set up a jewellery business there. Being the youngest in her family, Mum was sent to school on the Isle of Wight in the 'old country' where most British colonial kids were educated. I know very little of my mother's activities after her education was completed. I believe she fell in love with a sailor who died from some ailment and I remember her describing what was apparently a terrible loss to her. She only ever spoke of this incident to me once.

On completion of his college course, Dad drifted down into South America where Dan McKie, Mum's brother-in-law, employed him. Uncle Dan managed cattle properties (*estancias*) for the Liebig's company, which was named after German chemist Baron von Liebig and a meat processing plant was established in the town of Fray Bentos in Southwest Uruguay. It was here that Fray Bentos meat spread first saw the light of day and meat packing, both frozen and canned, was still the major industry of the town at time of writing.

At some stage in their travels, boy met girl when mother visited her sister, Penelope McKie. In spite of the fact my father almost drowned himself and his horse crossing a swollen river with my mother riding another horse close behind him, he survived to marry this attractive young

Chapter 1 In the beginning

My parents Mike and Jo's wedding in estancia garden Argentine

woman. The wedding reception was held in the homestead garden, a procedure that I was to repeat myself many years later on the other side of the world.

My oldest brother, Andrew Frederick was the first to bless this happy union, arriving on 23 January 1943. Nicholas Samuel joined them on 10 August 1946. Both being over 10 lb at birth, mother decided she'd done her bit for world population and was done. However, accidents happen and I arrived on 9 October 1949. The fact I was a girl may have helped my mother accept another child although I got the feeling that she had studiously tried to avoid it. Also, I was only nine and a half pounds at birth.

Hames family leaving Argentine L-R 2nd eldest Nicholas, Val, Mum, eldest brother Andrew.

Tensions were beginning to rise in the Argentine at this time. Britain had pulled out, retaining only the Falkland Islands in their control and the political scene was considered unstable and unsafe. My parents decided it was time to leave before they were forced into the armed services but in order to do this, Dad had to leave Liebig's Pty Ltd. Once settled in England, Dad rented farms in an all-out effort to make a living for his young family. I can only remember two of them.

My fondest memories come from the farm in Wales. I have no idea how its name was spelled because Welsh names are impossible to read, write or pronounce, but Blaenglyn (pronounced 'Bline glin') will suffice. It was situated

Chapter 1 In the beginning

I start out in animal husbandry at Blaenglyn, Wales.

amongst rocky rolling hills with a large stone farmhouse that had a flight of stone steps to the upstairs quarters. One of my more colourful memories of this place was falling down those formidable stairs. Not content to just plop down two or three, I tumbled from top to bottom, wailing like an ambulance. No doubt I picked up a few bruises on the way down but it was my pride that copped the worst of it and I was thankful Cousin Willy hadn't been there to witness my humiliation. He was my mother's nephew, Auntie Pen's son and my introduction to what I think we call 'bullying' today.

Me outside Blaenglyn farm house about 2 years old.

For some obscure reason, I hated anyone looking at my bare legs. In hindsight, this was unusual because most small children I know don't care much about such things and will happily scamper around completely naked. Willy quickly cottoned on to this in-built shyness and teased me unmercifully!

'I can see your legs,' he'd snicker and I'd bawl like a

Chapter 1 In the beginning

lost calf while desperately trying to conceal my chubby underpins from his smirking gaze. No sooner would I settle down than he'd say it again and off I'd go at the top of my voice once more.

As children in this home, we had to bath in a galvanised tub in front of the open fire. We all shared the same water so were lined up with the cleanest first while the dirtiest brought up the tail. I think the water was probably heated in large kettles on the wood stove, having no recollection of running hot water. I don't remember us having a proper bathroom either, but I do remember a very large empty room with a toilet in one corner that was marginally shorter than me and big enough to swallow me whole, which I was sure it was going to do. Mum used to sit me on this 'monster' that gargled and swilled everything into oblivion and I would desperately hold myself up, rigid with fear. I had often watched the toilet being flushed and dreaded that I might one day accidentally fall in and be flushed away with the poo too. Mum always waited patiently for me but one day, Dad called from downstairs so she walked to the door to talk to him. I don't know how long she talked, but it was long enough for me to tire and I let go, dropping into the toilet bowl. I believed my worst nightmare had caught up with me! With arms and legs pressed against my face, hands and feet sticking out the top and chubby bum wedged firmly in the bowl, I screamed fit to bust. Mother rescued me but she didn't look or sound the least bit perturbed by my ordeal. On the other hand, I felt sure I would be scarred for life, not just by the horrifying ordeal but also by my mother's apparent lack of concern.

The kitchen at Blaenglyn used to play an important role during our time on this farm, not just to feed us but to resuscitate 'dead' lambs as well. Sheep are known to be stupid creatures and my dad had to go out each day to dig newborn lambs out of snowdrifts. They were frozen quite stiff and showed no sign of life, but an hour next to the fire in the kitchen brought about a wondrous transformation. They'd begin to twitch and it wouldn't be long before the kitchen was filled with the bleating of hungry lambs. It was remarkable and I figured that what sheep lack in the brain department, they made up for with an exceptionally hardy constitution. I don't remember what used to happen once the lambs were rescued, but I suppose Father returned them to their dams.

My two brothers must have been tough kids too, like the lambs, because they had to walk over 3 km to school each day from Blaenglyn in foul weather or fair. Then they had to do it all again when school was over. I didn't believe this until later in life when I saw for myself. It was often the only way they could get to school as the luxury of school buses was uncommon at that time. Besides, the road was often impassable due to icy conditions.

The second farm I remember was a place called Weaveland in Wiltshire. It was here I learned about electric

Chapter 1 In the beginning

fences and riding pigs, both my father's doings. An electric wire was strung out a few inches off the ground to stop rabbits and father told me if I touched it with a piece of grass, it wouldn't hurt me. Trusting him implicitly, I took my bit of grass and promptly found out that electric fences do 'hurt', with or without grass. The fact I perhaps misheard the instructions was irrelevant. My dad was not a nice man for the rest of the day. Dad also placed me on the back of a quiet pig one day. He held me on but something went awry and the pig did a runner. Dad lost hold of me and I crash-landed in the slops. I grew to love pigs very much, but I have never lost my fear and uncertainty with electric fences. Especially after being 'bitten' by electric fences in several locations, both geographical and physical.

My brothers appeared to enjoy less 'painful' fun at Weaveland than I did. They used to climb on a shed near a public pathway and throw berries at innocent and unsuspecting pedestrians. Sometimes they would take me with them and we'd lie very low and quiet, surrounded by thicket. It was fun to watch the reactions of the targets but I suspect one of them informed my parents. That more than likely turned out to be a painful experience for the boys as such behaviour in our childhood was frowned on in the good old-fashioned way. We were seldom sent to stand in the corner.

I was about five years old when Dad decided he'd struggled long enough trying to farm for himself. One had to be 'landed gentry' or Lord 'somebody or other' with a huge inheritance to farm successfully in the UK back then, and we were in neither camp so Dad reapplied for a job with his old company, Liebig's. The company's headquarters were based in London and Uncle Dan was now one of the board members or CEO. I think he may have been a director.

Uncle Dan told Dad there was a vacancy on a Liebig's property for him, but he would have to leave England again.

'And where will I be going this time?' my father asked.

'Africa,' Uncle Dan said. 'Southern Rhodesia.'

I don't know how my parents viewed this new adventure. Dad had always been a 'pioneering spirit' from an early age but mother had only travelled to distant lands in the wake of someone else — first her parents and then her husband. I'm sure she was apprehensive as she packed my father's necessities in readiness for the journey. She would be leaving her ageing parents and all that was familiar to her for deepest, darkest Africa where lions were thought to roam the streets, but she put on a brave face and we children never suspected that she was uncertain or afraid. Besides, there were no streets where we were heading but we didn't know that then.

I don't know what sort of journey my father experienced as he travelled to his new job several months ahead of us in order to get our home prepared but I will never forget our trip. Neither did my poor mother! Travelling to a destination whose name she'd never heard of with three

Chapter 1 In the beginning

very young children in tow and no support is difficult enough today but our flight took three days and it must have been horrifying for Mum. She woke us very early the morning we were to leave. It was still dark and I was beside myself with excitement.

'Mummy, have you got a box?' I asked her.

'I think I can find one,' she replied. 'What do you want it for?'

'I want to put some clouds in it for the people in Africa,' I replied. 'They may not have ever seen clouds.' I wasn't to know that, like Australia, Africa is a land of droughts intercepted by a good rainy season here and there so clouds can be scarce and are always welcomed when they come. My generosity could hardly be called generous though, considering England was cloud-covered most of the time and rain was so abundant it was boring.

Our plane was a four-engine Dakota with propellers instead of jet engines, bumpy, noisy and flying very close to the earth's surface. One could see the white caps on the waves in the sea, impossible in our modern airliners at many thousands of metres. Of course, having no concept of death or tangled airplane wreckages, this was very exciting for me and I spent many of my waking hours bouncing up and down and yelling at the top of my voice, 'We're going to crash! We are going to CRASH!' This couldn't have been very encouraging for the rest of the passengers, many of whom were suffering from various degrees of travel sickness and I'm sure thoughts of murder were germinating in their minds!

When we finally stepped out of our plane into the blazing, white-hot heat at Bulawayo airport, Dad was waiting for us in a shiny black Consul motor car. I think it was new, but even if it wasn't, it was the most splendid vehicle we'd ever had though we quickly learned black wasn't a good colour in such a hot climate. Without the luxury of air conditioners, we travelled with the windows wound down. Even then we slowly basted in our own juices.

Two hundred and sixty kilometres south of Bulawayo, 100 km north of the Southern Rhodesia/South African border and a good three hours later, we pulled up in front of a big brick house, whitewashed on the outside with a red roof. This was our new home. The floors were polished red or green cement and we spent many a scorching afternoon's siesta spread-eagled on the cool concrete in our underwear. This was the Liebig's cattle property, always called Towla Ranch and so named from a big double-peaked mountain about 9 km away. My brothers and I only climbed that mountain once. The boys argued all the way up and down and I, being outnumbered, outsized and piggy in the middle, considered discretion essential to my well-being so remained unusually quiet.

Dad's new job was that of section manager of the headquarters section. Towla was a very large property, around 607,000 hectares in all. It was divided into

Our house on Towla Ranch, S Rhodesia.

Towla Mountain on the ranch, S Rhodesia.

Me and mum with orphaned baby elephant.

substantial blocks called sections and each section had its own manager. The headquarters section consisted of the ranch manager's house at the top of the granite kopje, or *dwala* as it was called, the clubhouse with its thatched roof and pool table, men's quarters, the mechanic's house, office personnel's residence, our house, the office, the workshop, various storage sheds, the store, the meat house and killing pens, the veterinary laboratory and just a little further away, the stables and cattle yards. We ranch kids used to congregate around the killing pen every week to watch the weekly butchering job that was to provide us and the African labourers with beef. It was here we ghoulishly dug around in the guts and dissected eyeballs, perhaps

Chapter 1 In the beginning

instrumental in leading me to a deep interest in biology later down the track.

When we first arrived at Towla, the beef herd was comprised mainly of Afrikander cattle. Wiry and tough but lacking the sort of conformation a good cattleman would desire, full blood Brahmans were eventually imported from North America and over the years, the Afrikander was phased out. Dad was made Brahman stud manager and we children engaged in a lively introduction to the art of leading cattle. Dad would break in the young animals he thought had show-potential and we kids would often join the morning 'crocodile', a line of young stud animals being led around the headquarters for practice. On several occasions, the scenery passed at surprising speed as a

My initiation into showing cattle.

skittish young calf tore away and dragged us in its wake. I seem to remember getting a snake's-eye view of quite a lot of the country this way as I was clumsy and the one who most often lost their footing during the 'drag' race.

Liebig's also owned a meat-canning factory at West Nicholson, 96 km to our north, and most of our cattle supplied that abattoir. Not content with just turning out corned beef and always looking for new markets, it was decided the ranch would breed pigs and the abattoir would create a pork and beef product. Because my father loved pigs, the job of managing this enterprise was allocated to him as well. Old unused piggeries were resurrected while others were constructed and it was here that I learned to really love pigs, forgetting the wild ride back at Weaveland. It was to the pigs I would turn when Mum and I argued, which was quite frequently in my teenage years and I would sit in a sty and play with piglets until my grumpy mood dissipated. I could never walk away from them without a smile on my face for pigs are God's real comedians. And how did my mum relieve her angst? I don't know, but being a mother myself now, I suspect she probably cried a lot — a less painful way to deal with recalcitrant teenagers than beating the head against a wall.

It was at one of these piggeries that I had a nasty encounter with a big black dog belonging to an African labourer. I was five years old and loved 'puppies' so when I came across this one lying peacefully in the shade, I stopped to make

Chapter 1 In the beginning

friends. It opened its malevolent yellow eyes and stared at me. When I persisted in my efforts to be friendly, it got to its feet and approached me as if it were stalking something, which in hindsight it was. Too young to read the sinister body language, I pushed my point.

'Nice doggy' I cooed but the animal told me clearly it had either misinterpreted what I said or it hated me anyway and it wasn't a 'nice doggy' at all. A throaty snarl and lips drawn back to reveal two rows of gleaming fangs convinced me that perhaps I should just let him go back to his snooze but it was too late for that. He had been aroused from his siesta and I was going to pay.

I stepped sideways — so did he. I stepped to the other side and he shadowed me, closing in all the while. With a skill not even seen in many sheep dogs, he mustered me into a corner. Without further ado or even a sound, he sank his fangs into my knee as far as they would go. As calmly as he came, he retreated back to the shade, leaving me standing in shock, two thick streams of dark blood running down my leg and tears coursing down my cheeks.

When I finally found my dad and sobbed out my story, pandemonium erupted. Because Africa has the dreaded rabies[1] included in its long list of exotic diseases, all dogs from that encampment had to be checked to ensure their rabies vaccinations were up to date. The culprit was located and I

---

1 An acute, infectious, usually fatal viral disease of the central nervous system transmitted by the bite of infected animals.

was fortunate that his vaccinations were current but so was he. Had they not been, it would have meant instant execution for him while I would have faced a barrage of multiple rabies needles in the stomach over a period of two weeks. My father and his workers endured a course of these needles when we had a rabies outbreak years later and they all said it might have been better to die. I think they were only joking, but by all accounts, rabies needles are notoriously painful. My understanding was that they had to be administered in the stomach to keep the vaccine away from major arteries and nerves. This caused bellies to swell and blaze red like the setting sun on a dusty African plain and no one felt like doing much for the duration of the course.

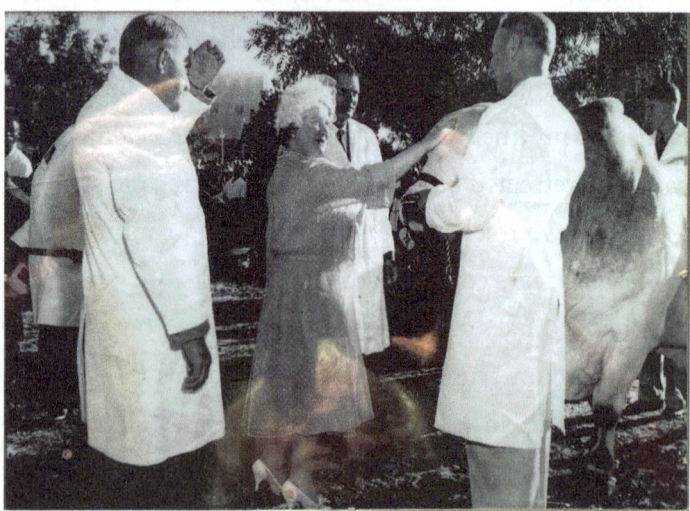

The Queen Mother presenting Grand Champion Brahman bull exhibit to my Dad, Bulawayo Royal show, Rhodesia. My brother Andrew on the right in the background.

CHAPTER 2

Growing up

Growing up in Africa, I had the best life a child could wish for but all my school days were spent at boarding school since we had no schools closer than 120 km away and this was the only negative for me. I would far sooner have been home riding my faithful old horse, Hilton, who was the culmination of years of wheedling and pleading with my parents to buy me a horse to call my own. I'll never forget the day my dad asked me if I wanted to go to West Nicholson with him to get something off the train. He kept me in suspense all the way so I was beside myself with excitement when a very plain and rather thin horse with a big head trundled off the stock wagon and my dad told me he was mine to keep!

My first taste of school was through correspondence. This was called kindergarten and it was at this time I was taught to read and write by my long-suffering mother. It was also discovered I had a talent for reading. Since Mum had plenty of time on her hands, she could read stories to me almost whenever I asked her to and I would sit on her knee and trace my finger along the words, memorising them. Then I would try to read the book by myself. Before I started primary school, Mum had joined me to a library that sent books by mail to isolated people and I 'gobbled' up as many books in a week as I could. Enid Blyton and *The Secret Seven* were my favourites, along with anything that told stories about horses. These were not the sorts of books one might have expected a five- or six-year-old to be reading.

Next, I was off to a little junior[2] school in the small township of Gwanda, 128 km or so north. It was here at St Christopher's that I discovered an inclination for drama. In my first year my mum signed me up to learn the piano, but at that time I wasn't musically motivated at all. Mrs Perkins was my teacher, a dear old lady very much in her twilight years and as sweet as she was, any musical aptitude that might have been lying dormant was destroyed completely under her tuition. She loved to whistle piercingly and shredded my eardrum every tune I played, a distraction my lack of talent could have done without. I was equally spellbound and repulsed by the copious amounts of spittle her tongue would apply liberally to her wrinkled lips so

---

2   Primary school

Chapter 2 Growing up

The daily milk delivery at St. Christophers primary boarding school in Gwanda, S. Rhodesia.

she could whistle properly and not embarrass herself by dwindling into a *pwhhhhht* sound, which was all I could manage myself at that time. I assumed she had false teeth and marvelled that she was able to keep them under control during the exercise. Under her tuition I was unable to grasp the art of reading music so I learned each piece off by heart. When time came to perform at the Eisteddfod, I managed to make myself look reasonably professional by glancing at the music and nodding each time my page-turner was to turn the pages for me, but not one note could I read. I thought I had them fooled, but I never won any prizes so I probably didn't.

One of St Christopher's school principals loved to produce musicals and I discovered a great delight in acting.

Mr Simmons produced two three-hour musicals and cast me into major parts in both of them. The fact my roles involved the equivalent of a village idiot in *Once aboard the Lugger* and the frumpy old Widow Twanky who tried to 'get off' with the Spirit of the Lamp in *Aladdin of the Underground* didn't concern me at all. Both parts were great fun and being young and impressionable, I enjoyed the accolades for my performances in the local newspapers the following week. It was probably here I decided my future lay in Hollywood. I would be a star!

It wasn't until many years later that I received photos of St Christopher's from David Adams. He was one of my favourite teachers and also married to Ann, Towla manager John Vavasour's eldest daughter. They eventually moved to Australia.

Their photos brought back memories that were buried too deep for me to retrieve on my own. However, I do remember the dress I was wearing in one group photo and I also remember how milk used to be delivered to the school by donkey cart. Of course, that was no big deal for us back in those days as donkey carts were one of the Africans' main sources of transport at that time. The other was the bicycle.

I was also reminded of my first real experiences with 'bullying' when Caroline, my primary school nemesis stared at me out of one of the group photos. Compared to Caroline, cousin Willy was a darling! Caroline was a very large child

St. Christopher's class photo.
My nemesis, Caroline on the right.

and I have unpleasant recollections of her throwing me on the floor and settling her corpulent bottom on my head. Adding insult to injury, she chose that moment to pass wind! I also reluctantly recalled being 'sent to Coventry' because I didn't choose to comply with a little gang of girls who took it on themselves to rule the roost. This practice effectively isolated a person from everybody else and even though I was still surrounded by other children, no one spoke to me and I would find myself sitting alone over lunch break.

As such a young child at boarding school, holidays were always a happy occasion and because St Christopher's was only 129 km from home, I was able to return to the ranch for long weekends. Much of my holiday time was taken up riding my beloved, roman-nosed Hilton through the African bush, stalking and getting as close to herds of beautiful wildlife as I possibly could. I would admire the stately *kudu* and pause to tease a chameleon, fascinated by its changing colours and its painfully slow tread. When not riding, I would join the other 'ranch kids' beside the swimming pool that had been blasted out of the basalt rock or *dwala* on which most of our houses were built. Rough though it might have been, we kids used to think we couldn't survive the hot summer months without it.

As a child who was prone to serious ear problems, I had the opportunity to test that theory on one occasion. Where there had once been soft dirt, large basalt rocks

Me riding one of the ranch horses, Call Boy.

were placed against the wall around the pool on which we kids used to lie and sunbake. It had now become a dangerous place, especially for children, and Mum warned the three of us that we were no longer allowed to lie or even walk on the pool wall. Unfortunately, old habits die hard. I forgot her instruction and I chose a bad time to be forgetful because we had visitors staying. I remember their son Jeremy, with whom I am now Facebook friends, as a little boy with freckles and prominent ears and as luck would have it, he lay in wait to catch me disobeying my mother's orders.

'I saw yer,' he chortled gleefully. 'I'm gunna tell your mother on you!'

I madly hoped he wouldn't because I knew what my mother would do but he did and that put mother in a spot. A stickler for consistency, she had no option but to punish me and I was given the choice of a spanking or no swimming for three weeks. No swimming? For *three* weeks? In the Christmas holidays when every living creature sprawled motionless on the coolest available surface to keep their temperatures down?

I loathed the thought of being spanked because my mum had a flair in that direction. She had relieved my father of this duty a long time before while we were still at Blaenglyn when she caught him 'patting' our bottoms and saw the smiles on our faces after he set us free. After some gut-wrenching deliberation, I settled for the spanking. The pain would be gone by nightfall and I could swim again tomorrow. Three weeks of intense heat without a pool to fall into would be more than I could tolerate.

Mum administered the cane, a bamboo riding crop with a bone handle, with her usual fervour. Cursing Jeremy under her breath with every stroke, which was some consolation to me, I was free to swim on the morrow. Oh, what a feeling!

I woke the next morning surrounded by a curious silence. Looking down, I discovered my pillow quite liberally stained with blood. While I never discovered what had happened, I was taken immediately to hospital in Bulawayo 250 km away almost completely deaf and with the threat of rupturing eardrums. Released a week later, I was prohibited from swimming for six weeks and I discovered a kid *could* survive the hot summer without the pool, albeit with greatest reluctance. My poor mother experienced pangs of remorse for many months after that even though it wasn't her fault. I wondered if the regret may have been more over the fact that she hadn't given Jeremy a good clip under the ear for telling tales! After five years at Gwanda, I graduated to Evelyn Girls Senior School[3] in Bulawayo. This school was comprised of over 1,000 pupils and I was now 250 km from home. The weaning process was well underway!

I hated Evelyn! Many of the students were boarders like me, incarcerated in boarding hostels that resembled prisons,

---

3   High school

big ugly square edifices of red brick. I don't remember much favourable about the inside either and the food matched the buildings — prison rations! It used to annoy me when my parents would both comment on how well I looked when my schoolmates and I filled up on bread due to what we perceived to be the poor quality of the main meals. I've since learned Bear Grylls can look extraordinarily healthy eating decayed carcasses, maggots and scorpions so I'm grateful we at least had good bread and jam.

Northwood House was the name of my boarding residence and was dominated by a petite House Mistress named Miss Turner and a hugely obese Matron named Mrs Fourie. We girls nicknamed her 'Farty' Fourie and she was despised by even the saintliest in our midst. She was a tartar and if we were caught talking after lights out, she made us stand out in the open courtyard under the stars for two hours or more in our pyjamas until she decided we were sufficiently cold and tired to sleep without further discussions.

At the conclusion of my second year in this awful place, immediately prior to end-of-year exams, I became ill. The sick bay was apparently not an option at this important time so I continued to attend school each day, walking the one and a half kilometres or so in crocodile formation to get there. I would write my exam of the day and was then permitted to relax, but I still had to attend to my studies. My condition continued to deteriorate to the point where I could no longer walk the distance and Miss Turner, who was also a teacher, had to take me to school in her car. Vomiting frequently had made me weak and I had to be helped to my desk where I would sit with pen in hand staring vacantly at the walls. I couldn't muster the energy to write much more than my name and date at the top of the page in those last few exams. Needless to say, I failed them. When the last paper was handed in and having cleverly kept me alive for two weeks, 'Farty' popped me into the sick bay and called the doctor. It wouldn't have ruffled me much if the undertaker appeared at the door with a tape measure. I felt so sick by that time that I thought dying might be the better option!

The doctor didn't need to look closely to diagnose my condition. In fact, she only got as far as the sick room door. A sallow face with orange eyes gazed vacantly at her from the bed across the room, quite obviously the victim of Hepatitis A, more commonly called yellow jaundice.

'Get her to hospital as fast as you can,' she snapped at Mrs Fourie. I wondered if it wasn't a bit late for hospital, but 'Farty's' antiquated and venerable old jalopy, which got me to Bulawayo General Hospital at a speedy 48 km/h, was as close to a hearse as I was going to get that day.

Evelyn's headmistress, Miss Powell may have had a pang of conscience when she learned of my plight, or perhaps her visit to the hospital while I was there, was something she did on a regular basis. I remember her as a tall, rather imposing woman with curly grey hair and a haughty carriage and I won't easily forget how she swanned into the ward, her nose snootily pointed skywards, with a chubby little lady at her heels carrying all manner of little gifts, chocolates and the like. When she reached my bedside, she graciously handed me my gift while I gazed up her nostrils and the little fat lady tittered beside her. Did she wish me a speedy recovery? I don't remember but throughout the encounter, she refused to catch my eye.

Because Evelyn school came so close to killing me, or so we thought, my mother removed me from it with the grace and dignity of a badly startled horse and sent me to a Catholic Convent school in Pietersburg in the Transvaal state of South Africa. One of my ranch friends, who was expelled from Evelyn for sneaking out at night to a party after 'lock-down', had paved the way to St Pious for me (they'd make a saint of her one way or another!) It was through her recommendation that I decided I'd like to go there. A much smaller school than Evelyn, it comprised of both junior and senior grades and it was like family, she said.

While the nuns were strict and sticklers for discipline, they were also fair and compassionate and sick students were treated like royalty. However, there was one thing I found disagreeable about their health care. Each time any of us developed so much as a sniffle, they sent for the doctor and we were given penicillin injections. Knowing what we know now about immunity to antibiotics, this could have been a disastrous course of action but I'm sure my reluctance to be part of this ordeal was due to a certain

Mother Superior Sister Gracias, St Pious Convent school in Pietersburg, South Africa.

amount of 'needle phobia'. Thankfully, my overall excellent health kept me mostly free from this option.

I was happy at St Pious convent and completed my last four years of schooling without further incident. I made the B team in hockey, the B team in tennis and swam for my school, (probably also B) but my heart was never really tuned in to sport. My long legs duped everyone into believing there had to be some sporting ability lurking there, but I was much happier composing poetry and I loved Fridays when we were given an essay to write over the weekend. Eventually, the nuns made me write my essays in poetry in efforts to cultivate my lyrical abilities. They also decided I was to represent the school at a state speech competition on road safety.

I thought the nuns' method of selection for this event was unfair. They instructed us Grade 12 students to write a road safety essay from which they would choose the writer of the best entry to represent the convent. I don't think any student, including myself, had put pen to paper before the nuns approached me. Setting some boring-looking books on my desk they told me that I was 'the chosen one'. The books were full of facts and statistics on road safety — excruciatingly mind-numbing stuff which, in my opinion,

Accepting first prize for the speech competition on Road Safety.

was unlikely to have my audience riveted on the edge of their seats.

Perhaps I should have been flattered but I was irritated by this 'selection by stealth'. I felt convinced there were other girls who would be better suited for the task and who should at least have had a fair hearing. It wasn't to be, so I handed the books back and told the nuns with a respect I was far from feeling that if I had to do this speech, I would make up my own. My speech didn't contain a single fact or road safety statistic but was a hastily flung together wacky and wildly exaggerated perception of things that *might* happen to those who chose to ignore the road rules.

Competitors weren't permitted into the main auditorium to listen to the other speakers until their own speech had been delivered — to ensure no one could plagiarise from someone else's work, I suppose. Being my usual lucky self, I drew the short straw and was placed last in the line of nervously fidgeting contestants. Sitting outside the auditorium in the chill of early winter, clouds of butterflies shook their wings in the pit of my stomach. The second last speaker, a boy from our 'brother' school opposite the convent stood beside me the entire time, kicking my chair with his foot and constantly repeating over and over how he was certain he was going to win. Talk of a positive attitude, he had plenty of that. And he wasn't lacking in confidence either. What he was missing was the sensitivity and foresight to know he would be lucky

Chapter 2 Growing up

to survive before someone could pull me off him and lock me away where *he* would be safe! I managed to resist the temptation, thanks to the moral teachings the nuns drummed into us.

The ushers finally summoned the bragging boy in and I was left alone to ponder whether I should race out the door and disappear into the night. Too cold for that by far, I thought so I held my ground and at last, the attendant came out to get me. My heart wobbled drunkenly in my chest and I remember slowly peering around the door. My mouth was dry and sticky and my tongue felt like it had died and was in rigor mortis. When I saw the crowd, I grimaced and they laughed at me. I hadn't prayed that my nervousness would disappear as a good student in a Catholic school might be expected to do but had I done so, this would have been the answer. I felt myself relaxing and I approached the podium determined to enjoy myself and liven the show up if I could. A few minutes into my speech the audience were genuinely amused and I was having a wonderful time.

I didn't expect to win that competition so when my name was announced, my jaw unhinged and my mouth dropped open like the bucket on a front-end loader. I sat stunned until the spartan Sister Bride jabbed me in the ribs with one of her bony fingers.

'Go on Valerie! You've won. Go and get the prize ...' When I still didn't move, she became more succinct.

'*Move it!*' That was our Sister Bride. Never long on words,

*St Pious convent house mistress,
Sister Bride (Bridey).*

if she had been making speeches on road safety, it would probably have gone something like

'Just do 'em or *die!*'

The euphoria I felt over that win lasted a long time and I still remember it clearly. I was supposed to go on to the National Speech Competition later in the year, but it never eventuated and I later heard that the other schools in Pietersburg, all of which were Afrikaans-speaking, were

Chapter 2 Growing up

devastated that an English-speaking school had won the regional title. We were left to wonder if they had black-banned the rest of the competition.

Sister Bride was the Housemother. Like 'Farty' Fourie she was a prison officer in 'drag' but quite unlike 'Farty', she was thin with lips like two strips of bacon rind, a beaky nose and sharp blue eyes behind large, round wire-rimmed spectacles. She kept us girls under control with little effort and we respected her immensely but it took a while to get there. I think we were all scared to death of her really but none of us would own up to it. Similar to Northwood House, one of the house rules forbade talking in the dormitory after the lights went out at night. Of course, rules are made to be broken, especially by a gaggle of giggly girls but Sister Bride's acute hearing inevitably landed us in hot water. Like a wraith, we would never hear or see her approach in the dark, but suddenly the dormitory would be flooded with light.

'Who was talking?' Crickets![4]

'Own up or you'll all have to suffer the consequences.' More crickets.

'Very well. Out of bed, all of you.'

Once out and standing to attention beside our beds, Sister Bride would administer her discipline.

'You are to strip and remake your beds fifty times, and I mean *strip* the beds, to the mattresses. No short cutting

---

4   Dead silence!

because I'll be watching and if I catch you, you'll do another fifty.' If you ever have nothing to do one day, or are socially isolated by coronavirus and bored out of your brain, you might like to try this exercise. On completion of this boot camp task, we didn't feel like talking anymore and Sister Bride could retire peacefully to bed, no doubt with a smirk of satisfaction on her face.

As formidable as Sister Bride was, she had a good heart and as students matured, she became more approachable. Many times, she and I would have long discussions in the ablution block next to the dormitory where we senior students would sit up late to cram for exams. There wasn't a lot that you couldn't talk to 'Bridey' about at that hour of the night, but come the next morning, she'd be back on track as straight as a ramrod, barking orders to one and all.

It was St Pious convent that introduced me to my first corpse. One of the elderly nuns had died and it was customary for the bodies to be displayed in the chapel so that we could pay our last respects. Uncertain of just what to expect, I was pleasantly surprised when I gazed on the face of the deceased. Alive, she had been the wrinkliest person I had ever seen but in death, the wrinkles had all but disappeared and she looked much younger. Quite remarkable, I thought and I found there was nothing to fear in spite of the ghoulish stories about corpses and dead bodies that tend to circulate boarding school dormitories after dark. I did have a quiet chuckle to myself on reflection

Chapter 2 Growing up

of the ordeal as I imagined all that wrinkled skin gathered in a ponytail under her head!

It was also St Pious convent that initiated me into the art of 'bunking'[5] out of the school grounds at night and 'bog-rolling' the Catholic boy's college over the road. For those not familiar with the term, bog-rolling meant unravelling rolls of toilet paper all over the school grounds, decorating goal posts, benches and the likes. I think we call it vandalism now. I was a somewhat abnormal country girl quite useless at climbing trees. Since this was a necessary skill for a bog-rolling campaign at St Pious, I was positioned on the perimeter fence as one of the 'watchmen'. It was my job to whistle if anyone approached and I did with gusto. I had learned to whistle quite suddenly some years before while out riding a black mare belonging to Towla's manager. She'd become relaxed at the continuous *phhhht, phhhht* noises coming from her back until my whistling apparatus unexpectedly decided to come on board. It emitted an ear-splitting whistle the poor horse clearly wasn't expecting and she very nearly left me leg up in the dirt. It took me a few hundred metres to pull her up and calm her frazzled nerves.

St Pious Convent school sat in quite a large area of ground that comprised of hockey fields and other sporting facilities such as tennis courts and a swimming pool. A high wire netting fence surrounded the perimeter with barbed wire at the top bending inwards to prevent us from getting out.

---

5 Breaking out

However, in a flash of creativity, trees were planted close to the boundary on the inside, making it relatively easy for the more athletic students to scale the fence and drop down the other side. As the barbed wire faced in, returning to the school grounds was a lot easier.

A deep council ditch ran along the outside of the fence, approximately 2 metres from it. I remember well a night when one of our adventurers lost her footing as she dropped down into the outside world, stumbled and fell headlong into the ditch. She wasn't hurt but the noise she made was considerable and I was convinced Sister Bride would soon materialise out of the darkness like a white spectre, her long robes sailing behind her and we were going to face music like we'd *never* heard before! It didn't happen, and I recall things quietened down a little after that episode.

Something else I learned at this Catholic convent was that dogs could have rather disconcerting sexual problems. Dogs were always turning up in the school grounds because we would throw them our sandwich remains, or the whole sandwich if we didn't like what was on them. One friendly fellow had almost become a resident and it was he who got himself 'hitched' to a lady friend one day in the most awkward way. All was going well, much to the extreme, albeit somewhat embarrassed hilarity of a bunch of snickering teenage girls just coming to grips with such matters but disaster struck and the dogs were 'stuck'. Nobody, not even a country girl, had experience with this sort of thing or knew what to do about it. I actually found it a little confronting rather than funny as some of my friends did and wondered if humans shared the same problem. Just then, Sister Bridget, a sweet-natured 'innocent' came rushing out to see what the commotion was.

'Who tied the dogs' tails together?' she cried. 'Who tied those dogs' tails together?'

I had visions of poor Sister Bridget sitting at the feet of the Mother Superior, Sister Gracias, later that evening receiving what could have been her very first lesson on the birds and the bees! Or perhaps they both pored over large encyclopaedias in efforts to explain this bizarre phenomenon.

I clearly remember the last time I packed my bags to leave St Pious Convent. Matriculation was over! I had developed a bad case of sinusitis during the exam period, but thanks

Matriculation formal.

to the tender care of Sister Bride I was able to complete all my papers, unlike Evelyn. Sadness reduced us to tears as we said our 'goodbyes' and even the nuns wept. They always said we were their naughtiest class ever, so I'm not sure if theirs were tears of gratitude or sorrow. As the bus passed through the stone gateway, we waved until we lost sight of each other. It was a great little school and I heard it closed down a few years later, taken over by the South African Air force, which had a base in Pietersburg. Ah, yes. We wouldn't just miss this little school but also the handsome young men in air force uniforms who used to sneak into the convent grounds at night to talk to the senior girls as they hung out of the top story dormitory windows.

CHAPTER 3

Life beyond school

I was tense and difficult to live with as I waited for my matriculation results to arrive. I had come home to find my dear old friend the ugly Hilton had been savagely kicked on the foreleg by another horse resulting in the destruction of a major nerve and had been euthanised. The usual hormonal problems that plague teenage girls, the anxious wait for exam results and the loss of my beloved horse did nothing for my disposition. If my mum and I clashed regularly before, we both resorted to stony silence over this period. It was the only way to get through the day without upsetting the apple cart and I think we both disliked each other very much at that time! Dad was reasonably immune as he spent most of his daylight hours away at work. Mum copped the barrage and I know I dealt it out to her in buckets!

When the tell-tale official envelope arrived, I remember trembling hands as I tore it open. My heart hammered in my chest and my mouth was dryer than seasoned wood. I didn't want to look but there was no going back. I passed — not an A grade pass but creditably enough to be employable and the whoop of joy I unleashed echoed through the house, startling birds snoozing in the afternoon heat just outside the windows.

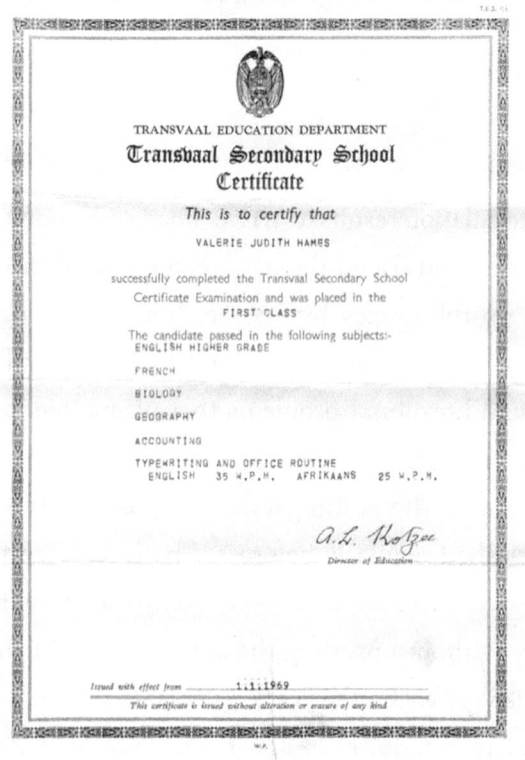

My matriculation certificate.

Chapter 3 Life beyond school

Job hunting was much easier in those days than it is now. While there were far fewer careers available to women in those days, positions were plentiful almost anywhere and the most difficult part was uprooting myself from the comforts of home to become gainfully employed. I think the fact Mum and I seemed destined to snarl at one another after very few weeks of each other's company more than likely played the key part in galvanising me into action.

My first job was as a library assistant in the Bulawayo town library. This was an imposing old building with thousands of books and as our first chore each day was to arrange all the books into alphabetical order, I soon became abnormally proficient with the alphabet. Where I used to have to start at a certain point like L to get to P, I was soon able to jump straight to the letter. My roommate told me I even recited the alphabet backwards in my sleep. Obviously, this isn't something I remember doing but I know I could never show off that new-found skill when I was awake.

I hated the library! Having developed a great love of reading and books from a tender age, I had thought it would be ideal for me. Perhaps it would have been different without Mr Stacey, the Chief Librarian. He and I couldn't see eye to eye and besides having to cope with his idiosyncrasies, there was an African assistant named Nelson who decided he didn't like me much either. Actually, he didn't like anyone much, especially if they were Caucasian. I can't remember doing anything that would have caused this antagonism but that doesn't necessarily make me guiltless. I believe these two people played a large part in my being sacked from the job. Mr Stacey obviously as he was the one that called me in and told me to look for work elsewhere, but I suspect Nelson played a more insidious role.

Money had been placed on the counter for me or a co-worker also named Val or little Val, to put in the cashbox. We were both busy at the time with two queues of patient people waiting to be served so it was another half hour before we were able to attend to it. In the meantime, someone picked it up from right under our noses while we were elsewhere occupied and the money vanished. Search as we might we never found it. Of course, little Val and I were thrown under the spotlight. She was a young married mother whom I couldn't see being the sort of person to steal money and I knew I hadn't taken it so my suspicion immediately sidled in Nelson's direction. In hindsight, this was probably unfair as I'm sure a customer could just as easily have lifted it but it wouldn't have surprised me if Nelson had taken it and laid the blame on us. Whether he had or hadn't, I think the day I walked out of the library for the last time was the only occasion I ever saw that man smile.

I had been unhappy at the library for a while and one of my friends had already left and was employed as a ground hostess for the Rhodesian airline Air Rhodesia at the Bulawayo airport. I'd always been fascinated by planes so I questioned Sue on whether she thought I could get a job

Chapter 3 Life beyond school

at the same place. She said there was no harm in trying and there were plenty of opportunities.

When Mr Stacey summonsed me to his office to tell me my services were no longer required because both 'little' Val and I were under suspicion for stealing the money, I told him I had already drafted my resignation. I'm not sure I really had. I think I was just saving face[6] but I had definitely made up my mind to leave and had indeed organised an interview with Air Rhodesia for the following week. I was so relieved to be away from the library I sometimes wondered if I recited the alphabet backwards the first night after I left the place.

I had to fly to Salisbury for my interview with the airline, Southern Rhodesia's capital city now named Harare. Air Rhodesia paid for my ticket and I returned to Bulawayo that afternoon jubilant, armed with my new Air Rhodesia uniform. I was ecstatic and the uniform was very smart. Not like the awful chocolate brown, box-pleated winter pinafore uniforms we had to endure at St Pious' convent. These were slim-fitting simple dresses of a beautiful turquoise-blue colour with a matching coat and smart beret-style hat. Navy blue shoes with sensible heels finished the attractive effect.

Becoming accustomed to shift work and airport life was traumatic to begin with. First, and most intimidating of all, there was Carl. Carl was my boss and, as white and undernourished as Mr Stacey had been, Carl was

---

6   Lying through my teeth!

big, rough and tanned. He was an Afrikaner (not to be confused with Afrikander cattle), a Boer (not to be muddled with the goat breed) somewhere in his mid-forties, perhaps even fifty. His face was round as a full moon with two of the coldest, blue eyes I'd ever seen that were capable of boring holes through one's body like a white-hot knife through butter! Not even a saint could accuse Carl of being a gentleman. If one was unlucky enough to get him offside, one had a very bad day ahead of them and that was all there was to it. Everyone else had a bad day as well as he would stomp and snort his way around the airport buildings grumping and bellowing at all and sundry like a buffalo with a head cold. The staff at Bulawayo airport were frightened of him and they accomplished with commendable speed whatever it took to avoid him. I doubt Carl would ever read this, but in case he does, I will add that this was the impression I had of him as the new lackey, cowering and scraping in his wake along with everyone else.

Carl and I plumbed the depths of each other's character quite unexpectedly about two weeks after I had started work for Air Rhodesia. It was also the day I learned to use the Roneo machine, which had been a mystery to me up until then. It was Monday, the day the Boeing from Johannesburg arrived and our little airport stretched and expanded under the hugely increased rush of humanity like some heavy-breathing organism. It was always a shock to staff that only catered for Viscounts hopping between towns in Southern Rhodesia for six days of the week. Life was relatively peaceful until Monday's Boeing passengers, almost as many in number as a normal full day's quota, ruptured the sleepy tranquillity. When an aircraft was to depart, a passenger list was typed on special paper and a lot of copies made via the Roneo machine. There had been no pressing need for me to learn to use Roneo until this awful Monday. I typed the lists and someone else copied them, but today was to be different. I was alone in the office when Carl came dashing in. He slapped the passenger manifest in front of me and asked me to whip off twenty copies. My guts tied themselves into knots as I approached the machine and gawked at it in silence. I searched high and low for some kind of button that might send it careening into motion, fervently hoping it would eventually reveal its secrets to me but of course it didn't. When Carl returned ten minutes later to find not even one copy, three fuses popped all at once and he roared with frustration and fury.

'What's wrong with you? You haven't done even one b ... copy!' he bawled. 'What the hell have you been doing? Sucking your thumb in the corner or something?' He should never have said that! Two weeks of walking on eggs around Carl had taken a greater toll on my nerves than I'd thought. My father's 'fight or flight' genes grabbed me by the throat like a brawling dog and shook me hard. I could almost hear him say in that distinctive way he had, 'You're *not* going to let him get away with this, are you, Stripey?' Stripey was a nickname attached to me long before I started school when Mum made me a pair of bottle-green trousers with thin grey stripes throughout and it stuck with me right to the end of my parents' lives.

'Well! If you had b ... well shown me how to use the b ... machine, you'd have had your b ... copies, wouldn't you?' I hollered back. Then I stormed out of the office to the check-in counter, face blazing with both anger and a ghastly fear that my new job was over before it had really begun. If there hadn't been so many passengers queuing up to check in for the flight to Johannesburg, I would have put my head down on the counter and wept.

The summons to Carl's office never came. I fully expected a terrifying tongue lashing for my insubordination and was certain I'd be fired. Instead, something quite extraordinary happened. Not a word was mentioned about the incident. Carl taught me to use the Roneo machine himself and his demeanour towards me changed 180 degrees. Dare I say it, we became friends ... of a sort. We could chat pleasantly together and when the leftover food from the planes was brought to the office, he would always bring me some if I were busy.

Amazement at this abrupt transformation of character doesn't come anywhere near to describing how I felt about all this. I was utterly confounded. I'm not in favour of having to yell back at someone who tries to cut me down just to win their respect. I'd never had to do it before but I felt my dad's personality had taken over the situation back then. His philosophy was to 'Never bear any resentment towards anyone but let 'em have both barrels until the breech is empty so they'll know you won't be gunned down without a fight. After you've finished, pick up the pieces and repair the holes.' From this time on, the staff unofficially appointed me as delegate if they wanted to impart some information or make some request to Carl.

During my two years at Bulawayo airport, I met many hundreds of people from every nation and walk of life in the world and discovered the true meaning of 'it takes all sorts'. Even in our small terminal, I came up against a broad cross-section of the good, the bad, the ugly and whatever else might fall in the cracks between. It was here I developed my fascination and enjoyment of people.

Several incidents, if they can all be called that, occurred in my time as a ground hostess. One was funny, one was tragic and one was the hardest lesson I've ever had to learn about personal relationships.

When travelling, many passengers would wind up in the airport bar and sometimes miss their boarding cues. Usually, they would hear the second call and sprint for the gate. Others, however, were either completely deaf or too inebriated to leave the security of the bar holding them upright and we would have to make several boarding calls. Planes were delayed and ground staff, pilots and airhostesses had their tolerance levels sorely tested on these occasions.

Our intercom had a switch that would transmit in either the up or down position but if using the down position, the switch had to be held. Let it go and it would flick back up by itself. If one used the up position, the switch remained in transmit mode and had to be manually switched off. Often, we would fool around when we made our announcements, making sure the switch was in the OFF position before adding some rude comment or noise and I guess it was only a matter of time before there was going to be a mishap.

I was becoming bored with making departure calls for one flight to Victoria Falls so, on the fifth 'final' call I pressed the switch down, bent my head to the mike and in the gentlest voice I could muster under the frustrating circumstances, I began my departure announcement again.

'Your attention please. This is the fifth and final departure call for Air Rhodesia Flight 213 to Victoria Falls. Would those passengers travelling on this flight please proceed immediately to Gate 5 for boarding'. I let the switch flick back up and yelled into the mike 'N O W!!!' To my horror, I heard my voice rocking the very foundations of the building. The switch had flicked right through the OFF position and up into transmit mode again. Chairs frantically scraped across the floor in the upstairs cafeteria and an avalanche of humanity cascaded down the steps and on to the boarding gate in a raging torrent. My Duty Officer Doug, a normally very nice red-haired and now red-faced man came bolting into the office where I cringed, gave me a withering look and said through tightly clenched teeth, 'I should fire you for this!' before scooting back out to calm the mass hysteria. He didn't and we were all able to laugh about it afterwards, especially as news filtered down from the restaurant of the overturned chairs and coffee spills on pristine white tablecloths. I ventured that perhaps we could do away with the four or five reminder calls and adopt my method, which they would have to admit was spectacularly effective. The proposal was resoundingly defeated.

I had other issues with that wretched transmitter, one of which was advertising a piece of lost property. It was a blue bootie off someone's baby and do you think I could get that right? My tongue cork-screwed around in my mouth while my brain lagged along behind and no one from the crowd was going to come forward and own up to having a blue baby who had lost a bootie! Nor did they understand what a 'boo blootie' was. I eventually got it worked out but for all the verbal gymnastics, no one came to claim the bootie.

The second incident personally affected me and clouded my life for a month after. As frequently used to happen, a doctor rang the terminal requesting urgent space on the next flight to Salisbury for a stretcher case. There were some procedures that had to be adopted for these cases and the doctor had not been able to comply due to the emergency of this situation. He became angry with me as I tried to explain the necessity of the relevant documents, so I handed him over to Duty Officer Doug.

In due course, an ambulance arrived and the passenger's name came up on the manifest I had to type and copy — Tom Jones. A Tom Jones worked on Towla Ranch and had become a very good friend of my family over the years but it wouldn't be him. Or would it? The name Jones is as common as tea leaves and 'Tom' wasn't that uncommon either. When I discovered that it *was* my friend, I didn't want to believe it and I spent several minutes talking to him in the ambulance before he was flown to Salisbury. He had woken up in the morning, stood up beside his bed as he'd done for forty years and collapsed for no medically identifiable reason. To my knowledge, the cause was never discovered and Tom became a paraplegic from that day until he died years later. I remember crying a lot over the following days. I loved Tom dearly; almost as a favourite uncle, he was quite a bit older than me and I couldn't bear thinking of him being condemned to a wheelchair all his life.

It's interesting that another resident from Towla, the mechanic's wife Val, suffered the same affliction. She also spent the rest of her life in a wheelchair and the cause for her collapse was never discovered either as far as I know. I suppose Rhodesia, being only a small country and out of step with Britain by illegally proclaiming independence from the 'mother land' couldn't afford the money to research this mysterious condition that smote two people

Chapter 3 Life beyond school

from the same area. It must have been difficult for their families, never to know if it was something that could have been avoided or something genetic which might catch up with the rest of them later.

And what of the 'hardest lesson' I ever had to learn concerning personal relationships? This was one of the few regrets I spoke about in my introduction and it still causes pain to think about it.

There was a man working as a radio operator at the Bulawayo airport we'll call Tino. When I first arrived, my friend Sue said, 'Tino will like you.' That didn't mean much until he introduced himself. Shorter than me and twenty-two years my senior, there was an indescribable sort of vibrancy about this fellow that I hadn't seen in anyone before. He drove a flashy red car and obviously relished the finer things of life. It was apparent he also had the money to treat himself to them.

Tino and I became friends and began dating but there was a nagging doubt in my mind that he was married and if not, at his age, why not? I asked everyone at the airport if Tino was married, but no one could tell me. I believe now that they knew all along but didn't want to become involved in a messy situation. They did me the greatest disservice! By the time I found out there was a 'Mrs Tino', albeit a very unhappy one, it was too late and our relationship had blossomed into what I naively thought was love.

This sad affair began to fall apart when Tino's wife rang

me and asked me to have coffee with her. I was stricken with fear, almost unable to breath but I agreed. She was very kind but told me in no uncertain terms that I was far too friendly with her husband and that I really wouldn't want her to be telling my parents now, would I?

She dropped me back at the girls' hostel where I was living and after I told Tino what had happened, I promptly descended into a depression that saw me lose 13 kg in one week. I stopped eating and the doctor prescribed medication that sedated me for twenty out of twenty-four hours a day. It was a *terrible* period of my life and for the two years that I worked at the airport the relationship staggered along going nowhere. I tried to end it (the relationship that is) on my twenty-first birthday, but Tino broke down and cried in front of me like a baby. I had never seen a man cry before and I had no idea what to do about it so I did nothing and we continued as a very troubled item. Troubled for me at least, because no matter how I tried, I knew there was something wrong with having a man so many years my senior. I couldn't help imagining myself aged forty and still active, with an 'old' sixty-year-old man in tow. (Of course, sixty-year-olds were very old to me then). I cried at least once every day we were together and I finally realised that to break it, I was going to have to run away. Literally.

In my second year at Bulawayo airport, I noticed a marked deterioration in my hearing. Having had so much trouble with my ears as a child, spending weeks at

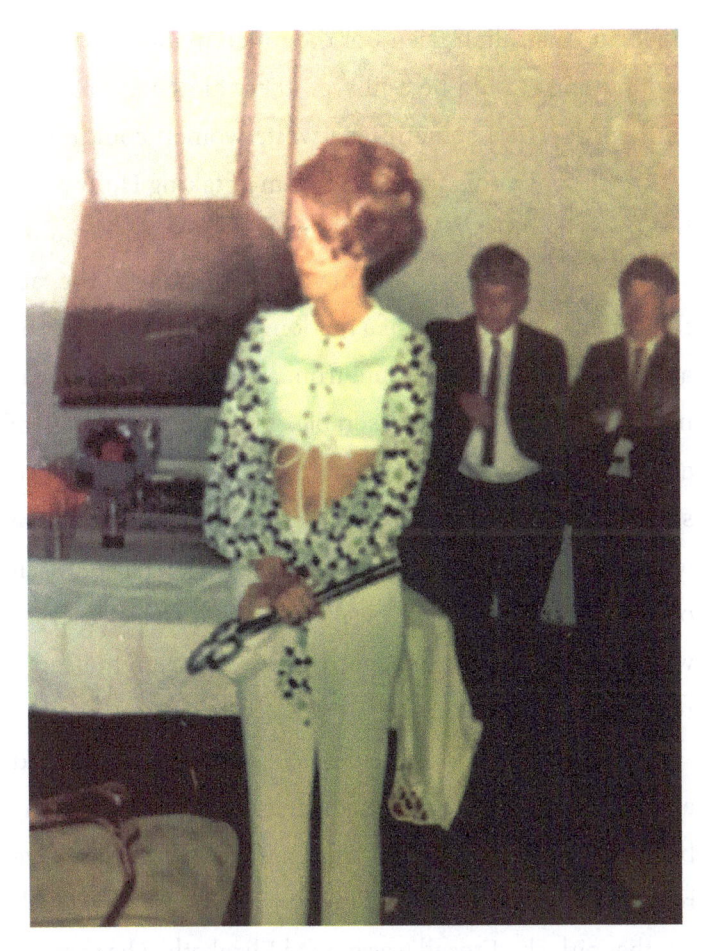

My 21st birthday party.

a time in hospital, I visited a specialist. It turned out to be unrelated to my childhood problems. The high-pitched whine of the Viscount engines was destroying the nerves and I was instructed to either leave the job soon or become totally deaf by the time I was thirty. The timing couldn't have been better. I had set my sights on going to Australia since an Australian friend of the ranch manager's family had told me I could be a Jillaroo there and work on large cattle properties, something a white woman couldn't do in Rhodesia. By this time, my dream of taking Hollywood by storm had dissolved in the mist of reality. I began to save up and had been for some time, oblivious to the fact the potential fulfillment of a life-long dream would also be a much-needed escape route from a relationship that was making me profoundly miserable. This took my mind off any regret I may have felt at having to leave a job I enjoyed so much and just before Christmas 1971, I said goodbye to Carl and the airport staff. I have only been back to visit once when Graeme and I travelled to Rhodesia just after we were married. Of the old guard, only June from the cargo room remained.

During my working life in Bulawayo, I found accommodation at a girl's boarding hostel. It wasn't long before I teamed up with a girl named Norma and we became roommates. She and I were good friends along with another girl who I recall was named Elizabeth. The three of us used to go out as a group and when we all had boyfriends, the six of us could always be found together. Then one day, Norma's boyfriend ended their romance and I have never seen another person quite so distressed. I worried about my friend after this happened. She would sit silently, staring blankly at the horizon, a freshly-lit cigarette dangling from her fingers. It was only when the cigarette had smouldered to the end and burnt her fingers that she would come back to us. I watched her many times mechanically flicking two inches of ash from her unsmoked cigarette and lighting another only to repeat the performance.

With the passage of time, when I was plotting my escape to the 'land down under', I persuaded Norma to come to Australia with me. She appeared excited at the prospect and we began to make plans but then she met Brian.

Sad to say, from the moment I met Brian I couldn't warm to him at all but he caught Norma fair and square on the rebound from her last love and I was soon embroiled in wedding plans and dress fittings, for I was to be her bridesmaid. She seemed so happy and while I was sad that she wasn't going to share my Australian adventure, it was refreshing to see her smile again.

Norma was married and remained at home while I travelled to Australia alone. It wasn't long before her letters revealed that the marriage was floundering and a year after the nuptials, it disintegrated altogether. It was around Christmas 1974 when I returned to Rhodesia with my new husband and included a visit with Norma. It turned out that Brian was wholly consumed by sport and Norma spent every night alone almost from the day of her wedding. She told me that she still wanted to come to Australia but it was very difficult for her to do so. However, she would keep trying and keep in touch.

I received a letter from her some years later saying she

Me on the left as bridesmaid to my friend Norma.

had to move to England for a time before she could come to Australia, so I expected to hear from her reasonably soon. Never the best of letter writers, I didn't hear from her again for years until a letter arrived to say she had, at last, landed in Australia! I immediately wrote back to her but never heard from her again. However, I met Norma just once more in the most remarkable of circumstances and since there are several people who dropped out of my life only to incredibly reappear at a later date, I have included a chapter on these remarkable reunions.

CHAPTER 4

Off to the 'land Down Under'

Early in the new year of 1972, I boarded the *HMS Canberra* bound for Australia. Because my parents were unable to take me to Durban to catch the boat, Tino took me. Being so emotional, he made it known that he would wait for me to come home at the end of the twelve months I'd planned to be away and we would be married. His divorce was either complete as he spoke, or was going to be. With a big yellow streak down my back, I couldn't bring myself to tell him that I would never marry him. He cried and I pretended as we hugged each other on the quay, but the sense of relief as I walked up the gangplank onto this floating hotel was overwhelming. Phase one was complete. Phase two would follow but I had no idea how upsetting that was going to be.

I was enthralled with this new seafaring environment, but as we drew away from the dock at Durban grief engulfed me. I stood at the back of the boat watching the South African coastline receding into the blue and thinking about my mum and dad. They had waved me goodbye from our house steps and it was the first time I had ever seen them with tears on their cheeks. It was gut-wrenching stuff and I cried like a baby at the back of that huge ship, an enormous weight of loneliness growing inside, wondering if it was too late and too far for me to swim back to shore!

As luck would have it, one of my cabinmates turned out to be my doctor's daughter whom I had never met. She and I and one other girl got along well together and it wasn't long before the young people on board had gravitated towards one another and forged new friendships. Our group did everything together, although 'everything' consisted mostly of lounging beside the pool during the day and dancing at the disco at night. We sometimes played table tennis, but apparently the pool and the disco must have been the main contenders for our patronage because I don't remember doing much else. I also read a lot on that trip and one of my favourite authors, Victoria Holt shared the journey with me. I purchased one of her books on board and she kindly signed it for me, along with many others of course.

Ship travel is enormous fun! We had a film crew board the ship at Perth to take shots for a movie they said they were making. We never did find out anything about the

Chapter 4 Off to the 'land Down Under'

movie, and I wonder if it wasn't a ruse so they could check out the 'chicks' but we gave them plenty of cheek. A few days later, I was disturbed from my snooze beside the pool by one of the film crew asking me if I would go up to the First Class pool to take footage there. Now, I had always wanted to be in the movies and my heart performed the perfect triple backflip, but coyness got in the way and I managed to stammer that I'd only go if my friends could come too. The man agreed and off we all went, clad in bikinis and beach towels. Except for me.

I had developed a severe bout of flu and had made efforts to see the ship's doctor. When I reached his surgery, there was a kilometre-long queue of people in front of me so I turned into my bunk, piled as many blankets on top of me as I could stand and sweated for a day or two. The day the film crew invited us to the First Class swimming pool, I was better but only just. My nose alarmingly resembled a juicy overripe pomegranate and while I still wore my bikini, I was also rugged up with a heavy winter coat.

It was a terrible day for filming pool scenes but one look at the First Class pool patrons clearly explained why we youngsters were being imported from the cattle class! Not many young people could afford First Class passage and let's face it, old people in bikinis were not exactly fodder for the movie industry back in those days. The wind whistled around the ship's double funnels and across the decks while thick clouds shrouded the sun altogether. The First Class pool was much windier than ours and as I walked down the steps to its deck, I wondered why anyone would want to waste film in such horrid conditions?

'Would you take off your coat love, and stand at the top of those steps there?' I looked round to see where the question was being directed and looked straight into the eyes of the director, or whatever he was.

'Who, me?' I inquired through my stuffy nose.

He nodded and I realised then it would be nothing short of a miracle if this little 'screen debut' would lead me to the halls of fame in Hollywood as I had once dreamed. Thank goodness I had got over my shyness about anyone seeing my legs!

I don't know how many times the scene was taken. My part was to walk down the steps to the pool as sexily as I could, doing the willowy blond bit, while two of my friends dived into the pool from different angles. After an hour of repeats, my friends were tired of repetitively diving in and climbing out of the pool and I was both bored and worn-out from climbing up and slinking down steps behind my swollen red nose!

At the precise moment we thought we'd got it right, a powerful gust of wind caught me in the back and blew my feet out from under me. I descended the steps on my backside as gracefully as I could manage, recalling the stone staircase at Blaenglyn on the way down. It was after this that the director decided to call it a day. We didn't see him again.

Chapter 4 Off to the 'land Down Under'

By the time I was due to disembark at Sydney, I had fallen in love with the sea and seriously considering becoming a stowaway. I had made friends with some of the ship's staff and was taken on clandestine tours into the bowels of the *HMS Canberra*, a strictly forbidden form of entertainment. If we had been caught, the guilty staff member would have been fired. I was sure making the 'bad guys' on ships walk the plank was pretty well out of vogue by then but would undoubtedly be the cheaper option; one less to feed and all that! Just thinking about it gave me incentive to keep my head down, mouth shut and eyes open.

On one of these trips, we ended up on the bows of the *Canberra* and the small group of us sat there quietly, right under the bridge and the captain's nose, watching the water rising above the railings as the prow carved through the waves on this darkest of nights. The stars were magnificently clear and reflected as tiny pinpoints on the blackness of the sea.

We chatted quietly about our 'welcome' at Melbourne. Just prior to our arrival there, the British had shot thirteen Irish soldiers, so the Australian Maritime Union decided to black-ban British ships. As a result, the *Canberra* wasn't permitted to berth to unload her passengers and some 450 travellers were disembarked and embarked via lifeboats, along with their entire luggage. Those who had vehicles on board had to make arrangements to have them returned from Sydney, where they would be unloaded. Passengers

*Unloading baggage at Melbourne after
Unions banned us from berthing.*

who wished to look at Melbourne were allowed to do so, riding in on the lifeboats. I didn't go for any other reason than I was afraid of literally missing the boat. The last place I wanted to be stuck was Melbourne because I didn't know a living soul there. All night long, our sleep was interrupted by the squeal of lifeboats being raised and lowered on grease-starved pulleys and I think we were all quite happy when the ship turned her nose seawards and we left Melbourne far behind.

Chapter 4 Off to the 'land Down Under'

It was on one of these covert visits to the ship's bow that I was first offered a 'joint' of marijuana. I was a cigarette smoker at the time, but I had developed a fear of marijuana because I believed it might lead me to more serious drug abuse. I really don't know where this dread came from. Drugs weren't an issue when I was growing up. Both my parents smoked tobacco and enjoyed the odd alcoholic beverage, very much in moderation, (except for the night my dad had to follow the pipeline home from the club house above our residence) but those were the only substances we knew about and our parents never taught us about smoking dope. Nor did the schools conduct any programmes. One used to occasionally hear that someone was smoking the stuff and that it was illegal. As a result, it was easy for me to refuse and no one tried to push it on me. Perhaps our position under the captain's nose and the illegality of it contributed to my safety.

I rose especially early on the morning we docked at Circular Quay in Sydney so I could watch the berthing procedure. The Opera House greeted our arrival, still under construction and not as readily identifiable with Australia as the Sydney Harbour Bridge. This enormous construction of steel brought home the message that we had arrived and I think we all held various feelings of sadness as we made our way down the gangway for the last time.

Customs took 'forever'. Whispers had passed around the ship that customs would be searching passengers for marijuana and I knew several people in my group of shipboard friends had brought some with them from South Africa. They must have been warned as they had tossed it over the side before docking but John B, who was in front of me in the queue, had every piece of his copious mountain of luggage turned inside out and diligently searched. They were so meticulous I thought they were going to take the stitching of the suitcases apart. I was relieved I had refused all attempts to get me to smoke 'dope' and I rested easy that I would be 'clean' through customs. I doubt I'd feel quite as easy now. I'd be worrying that others might have stashed some of their 'stuff' in my gear. That sort of thing didn't seem to happen back then, or we didn't hear about it.

Only one of my suitcases was searched. The officer re-fastened my case, smiled briefly and wished me an enjoyable stay before turning to the next passenger and I passed through into the bright Australian sunlight. Waiting so long for John's luggage to clear had given me tired feet and I was longing to sit down.

My next challenge was to get myself to Bowral, about 130 km from Sydney. The only son of Towla's manager, Jeremy and his Australian wife Joan lived there and I was to stay with them until I found my feet. Jeremy was about the same age as my brother Andrew and our families had been friends in the Argentine before we were all born. We grew up together in the Rhodesian bush, and now Jerry managed the King Ranch Quarter Horse/Santa Gertrudis

Chapter 4 Off to the 'land Down Under'

stud, although I think his responsibility lay mostly with the cattle.

Neither Jerry nor Joan had been able to meet me in Sydney, so it was left to me to find my way. Even though I was twenty-two years old, I was overwhelmed by this enormous city and with my hopeless sense of direction, I would definitely have got lost. Thankfully, big John B came to my rescue. Being an Australian and familiar with Sydney, he propelled me to the railway station and stayed to make sure I caught the right train to Bowral. I was so grateful for his assistance! One can only imagine how I felt, coming from a peaceful existence in the African backblocks to the hustle and bustle of Sydney town. I was quite able to identify with Banjo Patterson's *Man from Ironbark*, although I knew nothing about him back then. In addition to all this, I hadn't fully recovered from the flu and wasn't feeling completely well. I barked like a Rottweiler all day and this consumed a great deal of my energy reserves.

John hugged me warmly when we parted company. We had become good friends and it's never easy to say 'goodbye'. We promised to write to each other, which we did for a very short time, but he soon joined the ranks of those acquaintances I had made throughout my life and who had slipped into the shadows behind me. However, John was the second person who was to astonishingly re-appear on the scene many years later.

The train trip to Bowral was one of those unforgettable

experiences that pockmark one's life. The scenery was beautiful, but it wasn't this that made it a memorable trip. I couldn't be that lucky! This was the 'train trip from hell' and the driver was either a novice, inebriated or the Devil himself. Not in my wildest imaginings could I have dreamed that a vehicle running on silk-smooth steel tracks could buck so like a crazy horse with a burr under the saddle and a worm in the brain! This was no exaggeration as we passengers braced ourselves by putting our feet up on the opposite seat, trying not to dig our toes into somebody's thigh or between their knees. It was frightfully uncomfortable but surpassed the pain and/or embarrassment of either landing on the floor or having one's spinal column cruelly manipulated by the 'insane train'. It was the longest 130 km I think I've ever travelled.

I spent two weeks with Jeremy and Joan and their two adorable little girls, Kimble and Peta. I was to run into Kimble again twenty-five years later when she was dating the son of my future husband's best man, Tim. My life seems to be interspersed with several of these special reunions.

Jerry and Joan furnished me with appropriate newspapers to help me begin my search for work but as I had only one goal in mind, to work on the land, the *Queensland Country Life* was the most obvious place to look. From the age of twelve onwards, I had set my heart on large cattle stations. I wanted to be one of those silhouettes rounding up cattle in the dust, backed by a gorgeous fiery sunset. As with

Chapter 4 Off to the 'land Down Under'

most pipe dreams, the images I had of Australian stockmen were glamorised out of the realms of reality. Images of dirty, sweaty men hanging over rails coughing and hawking up great globules of dust-impregnated phlegm while swearing loudly at uncooperative stock would have been more truthful. The romantic version of the Aussie stockman didn't tell me they'd been in the saddle since four in the morning and their backsides were chafed and sore. Had it done so, my life just might have taken a very different turn!

After raking through 'Positions Vacant' for two weeks, I was becoming disheartened. No 'glamorous' Jillaroo jobs but there was a governess position advertised to teach a girl aged twelve and boy aged ten on a Northern Territory cattle station. I didn't want to be a governess because I had no faith in my ability to teach anyone anything except a bunch of bad habits. I wanted to be finished with school for good and I had never been any good at maths because I simply can't accept that some things 'just are'. No maths teacher I ever met could explain to me why a + b should equal 'c'. As for geometrical theorems, the fact they 'just are that way' and I had to learn them parrot fashion created insurmountable hurdles for me. How was I supposed to teach maths to Grade 5 and 7 students?

Joan, bless her heart, told me it was all very simple. The correspondence course we would follow made it almost impossible to misunderstand, she said, but then she didn't know of my lack of aptitude for mathematics! I told her I'd only ever passed one algebra exam in my life and that I had probably cheated!

'You'll be fine, I promise,' she assured me, so I rang the Brisbane number.

A man answered the phone and I introduced myself to him, making reference to his advertisement. His name was Lloyd and if they chose me, I would be teaching his children. He also managed Auvergne Station in the Northern Territory. After conversing for a few minutes, he told me I was hired and asked could I catch a plane to Brisbane to meet them as soon as possible as they were holidaying there and eager to return home. Eagle-sized butterflies soared up from the pit of my stomach into my throat, and my genetically erratic heart stuttered and bumped alarmingly. Through the deafening drum roll I heard myself saying something crazy like 'okay'.

Arrangements to travel were hurried and I took my leave of Jeremy and Joan at their Bowral home, not knowing I would only see them again once, not long after their son Simon was born.

I eyed the train suspiciously! It looked peaceful enough as it straddled the tracks, hissing gently in the hot sun but so had the last one. I wasn't looking forward to a repeat performance of the trip up, but I stopped short of interviewing the driver and smelling his breath! It was with great relief that he turned out to be skilled, sober and St Peter's cousin all rolled into one so the journey was blissfully

Chapter 4   Off to the 'land Down Under'

smooth. I enjoyed the lovely surrounds I'd missed in my effort to stay alive on the way up and I even managed to snatch a bit of shut-eye!

During the trip, I made friends with a girl my age and it turned out she was also due to fly that day, except she was going to Adelaide. On arriving at Sydney, we found the Ansett ticket office, checked on bus departure times to the airport and embarked on a window-shopping spree to fill in time, leaving our luggage at the town terminal.

When I left Rhodesia, we were in the middle of a bout of economic sanctions forced on us by the rest of the world. This had come about when we declared independence from Britain when Britain didn't want us to and it actually turned out to be quite a good thing for our country. Industries began to pop up that didn't exist before, and it wasn't long before we could produce the necessities of life without needing to rely on other countries to supply us. However, I didn't realise how much we didn't have in Rhodesia until I pressed my nose against the windows of David Jones. Common everyday items such as electric toasters and irons I had never seen before! 'Mrs Potts', driven by our reliable house boy and regularly reheated on the wood stove, always did our ironing and our toast was made either by putting the bread on a fork and holding it against the flames or by sitting it on a metal grill contraption above the flames. I didn't even know what an electric mixer was. Mum had always beaten everything with a wooden spoon or a fork. She later advanced to the hand-driven rotary beater. My ignorance of these items was not necessarily because they were unavailable in Rhodesia. Rather, my lack of interest in domestic matters could well have blinded me to these appliances, and as a big diesel engine provided Towla's electricity supply and only operated 6 am to 8 am and 5 pm to 10 pm each day, we learned to do without them.

My new friend and I caught a bus to the airport a little earlier than required and we had coffee together in the cafeteria until her flight was called. My flight to Brisbane departed half an hour later and I stared in amazement at the city of Sydney as we climbed above the clouds. Australia must be big if it could fit cities of this size in it, I thought, but years later I flew to London, and Sydney became little in comparison!

My new employers were waiting for me at Brisbane airport. Lloyd was short and stocky with dark hair. He cast his eyes over my skinny frame, and then grunted.

'You're not much of an advertisement for a beef property,' he said with a twinkle in his eye.

Lloyd's wife, Camille had been browsing when I had found the rest of her family. I was turned away, talking to my Grade 7 student Mandy, when I heard Camille's quiet voice at my left shoulder.

'Hello.'

Turning round, I looked down into a pair of the bluest

Chapter 4   Off to the 'land Down Under'

eyes I think I'd ever seen. Not cold, stony eyes like Air Rhodesia's Carl but warm and friendly.

Camille had a baby on her hip, which surprised me. I placed Camille somewhere in her forties, which I thought was a bit old to be having babies. Rebecca was the youngest addition to the family and either an after-thought or an accident, being about nine years younger than Mark, the second youngest family member. I suspect the latter might have been true. There were five children in all, but only four travelled with us, the second eldest being at boarding school. Neville, the oldest, was seventeen and had completed his schooling.

The trip to Darwin was uneventful but my first encounter with the Darwin heat in summer was not. As I stepped out of the cool interior of the aircraft, the high temperature hit me with a force that caused me to stagger slightly. Perspiration immediately ran in rivulets down my back and neck. I had thought Africa was hot and so it was, but nothing had prepared me for the assault of these searing and humid conditions!

We made our way to the air-conditioned comfort of the Darwin Airport, leaving Lloyd to seek out a light aircraft to hire for the trip to Auvergne. After some negotiation, he managed to charter a small eight-seater and we began the last leg of our trip 'home'. Auvergne was situated between Kununurra in West Australia and Katherine, NT and I didn't know then it was located next door to Bullo River

Station, home of author Sarah Henderson. Sarah wasn't an author at that time and when I met her, her husband Charles was still alive.

I'm not sure of the reasons, but Neville and I, both bigger than everyone else bar Lloyd, were relegated to two very small seats at the back of the plane. To say we were 'cosy' would misrepresent our real plight! There was no air circulating at the back and with the outside temperature standing at over 38 degrees Celsius, I began to feel quite ill. Neville didn't look so well either when I glanced at him, but I couldn't get a good look as my knees were pushed close to my face by the seat in front. It was impossible to turn to either side comfortably and the whole cramped situation hardly favoured wasting any energy wondering how someone else was feeling.

I remember thinking, 'This is it! I've come all these thousands of kilometres just to expire and breath my last in the back of a tiny plane and I haven't even had time to give anyone my parent's address and contact number. No one will know where I am and the only reminder that I existed at all in Australia will be a greasy stain on an aeroplane seat.' I cursed the *Queensland Country Life* for printing the advertisement and I cursed Joan's great faith in my abilities as a governess. And I cursed myself for being a sucker and believing her!

Fear of embarrassment prevented me from throwing up my dinner onto the children in front of me, but by the

Chapter 4 Off to the 'land Down Under'

time we touched down at Auvergne, I had begun to cramp quite painfully. This did help to distract my attention from a stomach hell-bent on eliminating its contents though. A gasp of fresh, hot air was sufficient and once I had managed to extricate myself from the 'torture chamber', the cramps disappeared. I was content to watch that little plane skim over the treetops on its return trip to Darwin and adamant that if it was left up to me, I would *never* make a trip like that one again.

CHAPTER 5

Auvergne Station

Auvergne Station homestead was a large double storey house and some fifty paces from the back door stood the schoolroom. This comprised of a shed divided in two by a curtain. The first half was the schoolroom and the second half my bedroom.

My room was comfortably furnished with all I would ever need — a bed, cane chair, table and cupboard. The shower and toilet were in a small separate shack about three paces from the 'schoolroom' door.

The schoolroom had a couple of school desks, teacher's desk and blackboard. The unit was quite comfortable and functional and a fan helped keep us relatively cool in the humidity. I doubt any of us would have survived without the fans.

Memories of my first morning at Auvergne are as

Auvergne station managers house.

clear today as the day itself. I was woken by the sound of hundreds of corellas screeching overhead, a frightening racket for one who had never heard the likes of it before and I leapt from my bed in a panic. Once accustomed to the din, the corellas woke me each morning in time for breakfast, which was handy as I didn't need to set an alarm clock.

Since it was still the Christmas holidays when I arrived at Auvergne, I was able to peruse the correspondence courses I was to teach the children. I spent a lot of time going through the maths lessons and was surprised that they were quite simple. I suppose they should have been, since it was only Grade 5 and 7 and not university entrance exams, but that doesn't mean a lot in my case. I was also allocated a horse to ride and Mandy and I would often ride together after school was done. It's a great way to see the country.

I hadn't been governess for very long before I was initiated to the Australian bush humour. Fumbling my way into my room just on dark one evening, I noticed a strange object hanging from the cord that was my light switch. Hesitantly, and thinking of gruesome tales I'd heard of objects hanging from light cords, I approached the mysterious attention-getter. I'd never seen anything like it before. Sort of oblong with two holes in it and surrounded by short, bristly hair, I could see a distinctive pattern of cells that indicated it was some sort of creature. The East Baines River passed very close to my door and because we were near enough to the sea to be affected by tides, I wondered if this was some kind of sea animal? Nothing in my memory bank rang any bells and when I figured it wasn't alive and therefore not going to leap at me with its bristles erect, I gingerly detached it from the cord and wandered over to the 'big house'.

'Could someone tell me what this is?' I asked the Fogarty family who were sprawled about in variously relaxed poses digesting their dinner. Seeing the alien object in my hands, as one they fell apart laughing. So great was their mirth they couldn't answer my question for a while until, wiping their eyes, they finally released the secret. They had killed

Chapter 5 Auvergne Station

a cow for meat (referred to as a 'killer') and someone had the bright idea to cut the animal's nose off and hang it on my light cord. Once I knew what it was, it was easily identifiable, but until one has actually stared up the nasal passages of a cow without a cow's head behind it, it's nigh on impossible to imagine how alien a cow's nose 'flying solo' actually looks. The following poem was penned in honour of that rather harrowing experience:

Won by a Nose with (a lot) of 'poetic license'
A new governess is coming — the bush kids paled with fright
And if she doesn't miss her plane she should be here tonight.
'We know what a governess means — she'll clip our wings for sure
And tie us down behind our desks and lock the school room door.'

'We're used to disappearing at the first faint light of day
And heading to the mustering camps where we join in the fray.
We crack our whips and strut about like all good stockmen do
But go to school? Don't be a fool! Our days at school are few.'

'We'll welcome our new governess with initiation rites.
We'll show her our bush humour far away from city lights
She'll get the biggest bleedin' fright that she'll have ever had
Don't be surprised if she heads bush ... now wouldn't that be sad?'

The governess came and settled in; the schoolroom was her home.
The children watched her every move right from the aerodrome.
And then a chance came waltzing by, too good to let it pass
Their father shot a cow for beef, the kids hid in the grass.

The governess wandered to her room in fast receding light
She reached out for the light cord but stopped dead at the sight
Of something she had never seen just hanging from that string
An alien creature with two holes — a hairy, slimy thing.

It took a while to figure out but then she realised
A fresh cow's nose hung from the string, it hadn't even dried
The kids had cut it off the beast their dad had killed before
And hung it in the teacher's room, then hid behind the door

The governess heard a scraping sound and realised what was up
She carefully took the cow's nose down and put it in a cup.
She washed it, sprinkled it with salt then to the noise she
   turned
Cut off a bit and swallowed it-her stomach fairly churned!

A sound of hurried scrambling came from behind the door
Little Ed came staggering out and fainted on the floor
Young Sally cried and scuttled past then stood with shoulders
   hunched
Without a sound she swivelled round and threw up all her
   lunch.

Chapter 5 Auvergne Station

Our governess had won the toss but paid an awful price
The contents of her stomach boiled and came up once or twice
Now years have passed and as she sits to watch the sunset's glows
She often thinks about that day when she 'won by a nose'.
© Val Wicks

Lloyd owned a few racehorses and his trainer was a little elderly, bow-legged fellow named Paddy. He didn't have an Irish accent but he reminded me of how I imagined an Irish leprechaun might look; short with bandy legs, gnarled hands and a weather-beaten hide covering his slight frame. Paddy and I got on well from the start and I would often help him with the racehorses, riding them in training. My skinny 175-centimetre structure in a jockey pad was no doubt something to see and many times, my mouth connected with one of my knees. I was never comfortable in this unnatural position, always felt vulnerable and vehemently hoped the horse beneath wouldn't think of executing so much as a crow hop, which would have certainly left me belly-up on the track. I was glad Paddy didn't make me use the 'pad' often.

Old Paddy abused the grog a bit, and sometimes he would roar at me, but generally our relationship was amicable. He used to like to train the horses by swimming them in the East Baines River, hitched to the back of a little rowing boat. I wasn't very keen on this operation because Paddy would make me row while he whispered sweet encouragement to the horse swimming along behind. I had never rowed a boat before and couldn't row for nuts but I learned quite quickly one day when the 'star of the stable' Moon Orbit swam faster than I could row and started trying to scramble into the back of the boat.

Paddy's encouragement was now divided equally between the horse and me.

'Whoa on, you little beauty. Don't hurry now,' to the horse.

'Get this b ... boat moving woman or he'll drown us all!' to me. My dad always said he wanted me to marry a man who put his flocks and herds first and me second. I don't remember thinking that was such a good idea but if I was going to have a weak moment, Paddy nipped it in the bud right there! In the following minutes I either became a very proficient rower or the horse tired because we made it safely to shore and not all of Paddy's sweet talking, which was limited to a few beautifully-enunciated Australian expletives, could coax me to go through it all again.

A lot of my spare time at Auvergne was spent with horses, either riding with Mandy or helping with the racing team. I only visited the stock camp once where the jackaroos[7] conducted the yearly mustering and branding. Having had a lifetime of experience with the quiet Towla cattle, I leaped into a yard full of big horny beasts one day to help push them up onto the waiting road train. After all, this was how we did it in Rhodesia.

---

7   Apprentice (trainee) stockmen

Chapter 5 Auvergne Station

Above the roar of bellowing cattle and cursing stockmen, I heard Lloyd singing out to me but 'singing' might not be the right word to use. I didn't understand what he was saying, but his wild gesticulations were plainly understood. They said something like 'Get your backside out of there, you dumb cow! They'll kill you!' I discovered later Australian cattle on vast tracts of land weren't like our cattle at home. They only saw a man once a year and sometimes not even then if they could avoid it. One couldn't walk out into the paddocks and scratch them behind the ears. Many were unbranded, or 'cleanskins' who had skirted around the musters for years and they were seldom in the mood to be sociable once they were behind yard rails. Hence, I learned a new set of values with regard to cattle handling. When Mandy and I rode through the bush, I remember being amazed at the number of dead cattle we would encounter on a trip. I must have sounded quite stupid because I would ask Mandy if her father was aware of their deaths.

Cattle-keeping records back at Towla were very precise. They had to be because it wasn't past the odd employee to steal an animal or two to add to the little herd that he was allowed to keep for himself on the property. Every paddock was numbered and a certain quantity of cattle were put in them. This record was then entered into the books. A couple of men were placed in charge of each paddock and they would be responsible for mustering the animals to be dipped at allotted times. These men would report each dead animal, the carcass would be inspected and then written off the books.

In Australia, it seemed that most of the large properties didn't know how many cattle they actually owned and because there were often no boundary fences to separate one station from another, mustering sometimes took in the neighbour's cattle. If the manager was honest, he'd notify the neighbour beforehand that he would be conducting a muster at a certain place, giving the neighbour time to organise a couple of stockmen to attend. Any of their branded cattle that had been caught up in the muster would then be drafted out and 'cleanskins' shared. On the other hand, if a manager was a shifty character, the muster wouldn't be advertised, the neighbour's branded cattle would be let go with perhaps a killer taken from them, and the clean skins quickly marked. How the property bookkeepers managed the tax returns remains a mystery. Perhaps they did keep records and if they didn't, I imagine the GST will have changed that.

I don't recall what my wages were as Auvergne's governess. I think it was around twenty dollars a week, but I was told I could earn an extra five dollars if I milked the cow every morning. I had never milked a cow before, but the extra money was sufficient incentive for me to give it a shot.

The following day, having risen with the screeching cockatoos, I walked up to the cow yard some 28 metres from the homestead. An old Aborigine was already there,

Chapter 5 Auvergne Station

complete with bucket and an old Shorthorn cow with a lot of white in her eye. Her calf was locked away from her and her miserly little udder showed signs of strain. Ned expertly baled her, secured her hind leg so she couldn't kick and squatted beneath her flank. Streams of milk squirted effortlessly into the bucket and I felt confident that I could do the job.

That cow and I very quickly reached the conclusion that we didn't think much of each other. She did everything she could to dodge me, both in the yard and out of it. When Mandy and I rode out each evening to bring her in, she would hide under acacia bushes, becoming almost invisible to the human eye. We decided to put a cowbell around her neck so that we would be able to hear her when she couldn't be seen but it didn't take her very long to work out that the bell was leading us to her. Quickly, the bell became silent. Mandy and I would comb the paddock from top to bottom looking for the cunning old bovine, mystified by the bell's stillness — until I bumped into her one afternoon.

I had dismounted from my horse in order to better fight my way through the thick tangle of scrub when I spotted her. She stood rigidly still, her neck extended. Not a muscle twitched, but as I moved into her range of vision, her eyes swivelled in my direction. It was the only evidence I had that she was still alive!

My milkmaid experience ended abruptly not long after it had begun, and so did the five extra dollars a week. The personality clash between the cow and me had escalated and I had watched in awe as she lay flat on her belly and crawled under the bottom wire of the fence, just to get away from me! As a result of the stress, her milk supply dwindled and my patience with it. Our last day together was the culmination of the most uneasy relationship I've ever had with any animal and a debacle to boot. The cow refused to let her milk down for me, so I put a rope around the calf's neck and let it at her to stimulate her maternal responses. It was a silly thing to do for two reasons. One, she had so little milk the calf would have guzzled the lot before I could (if I could) pull it away from her. Secondly, when I tried to shut it away again, the calf's vocal objections woke the entire station and it bolted round the yard with me in tow. On the second lap, I fell over a tree root and landed face down amongst the by-products of the cow's ruminations. One more circuit of the yard on my stomach and I decided it was time to let go.

No one told me my cow-milking days were over. I dutifully dragged myself out of bed with the cockatoos the next morning and I suppose the fact that I couldn't find the milk bucket should have warned me. I arrived at the yard to find old Ned squatted peacefully beside the cow. Butter wouldn't have melted in her mouth. She had won and I was five dollars a week poorer.

If I had thought I was to be just a governess at Auvergne, I was mistaken. As I'd already discovered, a governess can,

Chapter 5 Auvergne Station

and often does, have to turn her hand to many tasks. On one occasion, I was commissioned to paint the homestead roof, along with Alan the bookkeeper and Mark and Mandy. One of my other duties was to wash up the dinner dishes in the main house at night because I ate my meals with the family there. This routine comprised of my fetching the food from the kitchen on a trolley and then taking the remains back when we had finished. On my way back with the leftovers one night, in a very dark area, I decided I'd drink some of the left-over custard straight out of the jug. Not terribly hygienic and I hoped 'Cookie' wouldn't mix the leftovers in with fresh custard the next morning. The custard was thick and when I tipped the jug up, nothing happened. I tipped it a little further and still nothing. Then I gave the jug a gentle tap on the bottom and the custard let go, covering most of my face. Blinded and desperately hoping I wouldn't run into anyone, I groped my way to the toilet, which also had a basin in it, and washed the incriminating evidence away. No one ever did find out about that little 'flop'.

The second incident happened when I was on my way to the big house with the dinner. I was in a hurry and the paving on the veranda I had to traverse was pocked with holes. As I whistled around the corner at breakneck speed the trolley's wheel jammed in a hole and it came to a dead stop. Some of the food shot off the front and I sailed ungracefully over the top to join it. I picked it all up and rearranged it as best I could and I don't remember anyone commenting, although I did own up to that one.

In hindsight, I would have much preferred to eat with the rest of the station staff in the staff kitchen. I thought the Auvergne concept of a governess was a little old-fashioned, the governess being expected to live with the family most of the time. I had virtually no free time on my own as Mandy would want to ride with me in the afternoons after school, and while I understood her delight at having someone to ride with her, I often wished I could shut myself away from my students. The weekends were frequently spent taking the Aboriginal workers to a billabong or river to fish, and the Fogarty family would go along too. I felt I was expected to tag along, and while I enjoyed these outings very much, I longed for a break and time to socialise with the other staff who were more my age. I can honestly say that in my months at Auvergne, I hardly knew the cook at all, and I can only remember a couple of helicopter pilots. The stockmen were out at the stock camp most of the time.

I've already spoken a little of the 'jockey' job I was asked to do occasionally, only on the training track. I loved doing this and it was refreshing for me to fly around the track on a mountain of finely tuned muscle, feeling the wind ripping through my hair and hearing Paddy's shouts of encouragement or curses of disdain in the distance. As a small child, I had dreamed of riding racehorses and this was fulfilment enough for me. I was later thrilled to be able to ride in certain races at the Picnic race meetings that were held in various places around the country, and the adrenaline burst that came from winning only one of them was addictive.

Auvergne had two large water tanks set on high tank stands immediately behind the schoolroom. As a Jill of all trades, I shouldn't have been surprised when Camille asked me to help clean them out one day. To do this, I had to climb up about nine metres into the tanks that had been emptied the previous day to sweep the accumulated silt and filth off their bottoms. Whilst engaged in that task, water was pumped up so I could sluice the sludge out. Flying foxes used to drink from those tanks and I was somewhat daunted by the bloated corpses of a few who had drowned themselves in the rush. However, once I'd removed them, the job was enjoyable. Mandy gave me a hand and we had water fights from time to time if the heat became too much to bear. I only had to clean the tanks once.

Paddy tried to tutor me on how to shoe a horse. I gave it my best shot but didn't have the physical strength to do the job properly and decided immediately this was one trade I wouldn't be signing up for.

CHAPTER 6

Auvergne 'pets'

I suppose the 'milk cow from hell' must rate a mention in the list of Auvergne animal characters, though I could never look on her as a pet. Pest was the only printable description I had for her, but one had to admire her character and the ingenuity she portrayed in escaping from me. She certainly ranks as one of my more memorable animal acquaintances on that station.

There were two station pets in the true sense of the word. One was Lloyd and Camille's little dog who was short on legs but long on patience and good temperament and whose name evades me, and the other a Sulphur Crested Cockatoo with the original name of 'Cocky'. I was entranced by Cocky's magnificence the first day I arrived at the station and was determined to make friends. He was not so inclined. With persistence, I pursued this bird's affection until one day, he sank his great curved beak into the ball of my thumb while I was scratching his chest. My first impulse was to scream in agony and tear my hand away but I ground my teeth and, with a tremendous surge of willpower resisted the urge. Judging by the ferocity of Cocky's grip, my thumb might have stayed in his beak if I had.

I've no idea what chemical reaction this unpleasant exchange triggered in 'Bird Brain', but from then on, he would follow me wherever he could. If I were lying on the stretcher at the barbeque area, he would climb up and cuddle up to me with great affection. I began to gently tug his tail and then tip him up onto his beak and it seemed this activity met with as much approval as a dog shows when it's scratched on the butt of the tail. He never tried to bite me again. Perhaps I had shown my superiority by not yelling or flying away as another bird may have done in the wild and I had become the 'boss cocky' in his small world.

Auvergne had a herd of goats when I arrived there, and one Jenny donkey. I think she was named Jenny, very original, but I didn't get to know this beast of burden before it was banished to a distant paddock in disgrace. Quite unexpectedly, it waded into a group of baby goats intent on killing as many as it could. Nobody knew what had triggered this behaviour. Can lady donkeys have PMT? Regardless of the reason, two kids died that day and a third suffered two broken front legs. Mandy tearfully brought this poor little creature to me and my veterinary 'hormones'

Mandy and I riding closely tailed by the goat-destroying donkey.

L-R Bekky, Misfit the goat and Mandy, Auvergne.

Chapter 6   Auvergne 'pets'

leapt into action. Being only very young, the breaks were green-stick fractures so I decided to take this baby into my home in an attempt to heal it.

We named the kid 'Misfit'. One of triplets, and with goat mothers only having two teats, he was the undernourished third so it's possible he would have died anyway except for human intervention. Mandy helped me make splints for his legs. She also provided an old dolls cot for me to keep the kid in at night.

It was through Misfit that I had my first insight into how it must be to have a real baby to look after. I would bottle feed him and put him to sleep in the cot near my bed at night, only to be woken by his pitiful bleating a couple of hours later. Goats are intelligent creatures and when Misfit wet his bed, he would stand up at the end of the cot and cry until I woke up and changed the bedding. Then he'd lie down again, curl his little fluffy head into his flank and fall soundly asleep while I lay wide awake in the dark for the next half hour or more, wishing I'd never met him!

Misfit healed completely and I was finally able to release him back to the herd, not without a painful mixture of gratitude and sadness. He was a delightful pet and I had enjoyed caring for him but the broken nights were not conducive to being a good governess! Misfit grew into a large wether and the children and I would often have a chat with him when the mob was near the homestead.

There were many horses on Auvergne, station horses

that belonged to the Pastoral company, but Centurion was different. He was an ageing ex-racehorse who was reputed to have won some fairly big races in the north, although I never really established that, and he belonged to Lloyd's brother, George. Because I had proved I was able to ride a horse without being led, it was decided I could have Centurion for the period of my stay. He and I got along famously. He was spirited without being foolish, fast and had a keen sense of humour. Never was this more graphically displayed than when I was trying to catch him, but 'humorous' wasn't a description I would have given to his activities at the time.

Like lots of horses, Centurion loved bread and this is the incentive many riders use to coerce their mounts into submitting to the saddle. However, this horrible old nag quickly developed a plan. He would reach out, take the offered bread and then bolt away to the far end of the paddock with his tail held high over his back like a banner, tooting noisily as he went. I would trudge after him and offer him another piece of bread, only to have him repeat the whole performance again. This would continue until the bread was either all gone or had become a soggy lump of dough in my sweaty clenched fist. My blood pressure soared through the roof and my jaw muscles knotted with rage! When the pressure was at its most intense and I was ready to shoot the horse to catch him, Centurion would capitulate like a lamb being led to the slaughter (how I wished!) I'd walk up to him empty-handed, put the bridle on and lead

Chapter 6   Auvergne 'pets'

Painting the roof on the manager's house, Auvergne.

Auvergne stock camp.

him away to the saddle as if nothing had happened at all. Words can't describe the aggravation this little show of independence caused me!

Centurion only bucked me off once, but he and I did part company on other occasions as well. The day he bucked, I had finally caught up with him in the paddock and was attempting to mount him bareback. I never learned to leap onto a horse bareback and my father always told me I had as much spring as a 'bag of spuds'. The only way I could mount without stirrups to aid me was to lead the horse to a fallen log or take as big a jump as I could muster, dig my elbows into the horse's spine and drag myself up. This was neither pretty to watch nor easy to do but it worked for me, sort of. There was no fallen log on this particular day so I had to resort to the second method. I'd almost dragged myself the last few inches of the way when the large, garish buckle that adorned the belt I was wearing bit into Centurion's spine. Without further ado, he ungraciously dumped me on my back and departed with his nostrils flared, tail flying high and loudly snorting his disapproval at my incompetence. I couldn't bear the thought of having to go through the 'catching' routine again and asked Mandy to make sure his bridle was taken off.

Centurion and I occasionally parted company when we went jumping together. Mandy and I had constructed a jump out of 200-litre drums and poles. Centurion had obviously never jumped anything before that he could remember and while he was willing enough to try, he'd occasionally balk at the last minute. I had very little experience myself in this pursuit but discovered I could fly over the jump quite easily while he watched from the other side! However, the second most memorable occasion when I fell off the horse was after we'd been for a swim together and were walking around the training track in front of the house. George had accompanied me on another horse. He hadn't swum and was attired in proper riding gear. I, on the other hand, was perched on Centurion's bony spine in my swimming togs.

After walking for a while, we determined to liven the pace up a little and began to canter. As with most racehorses, Centurion only had three gears — stop, walk or flat gallop. Walking was apparently not an option that day so away we went. His mouth was as hard as tempered steel, and without the leverage of stirrups, the harder I pulled, the further up his neck I travelled. Of course, he headed off towards the river which was separated from us by a barbed wire fence. Approaching barbed wire fences bareback in swimming togs on an uncontrollable horse at full tilt is rather frightening, especially when one knows the horse can only do one of three things, but which? Centurion would either attempt to jump, which I doubted on the strength of our jumping lessons, duck to the right or veer to the left. I don't remember where I placed my bet but he read my mind and did the opposite, abruptly unloading me onto the barbed wire. The wire actually broke my fall, but the barbs broke my skin and it was only while I was riding the other horse home that I felt the sting on my backside and saw the blood.

Camille was horrified when she discovered what I'd done and demanded I go to the bathroom and remove my bathers. She liberally applied an antiseptic that I'm sure would have burned through steel and I remember bouncing around the bathroom, waving my hand around my rear end in an effort to cool the sting!

Next in line of animal friends at Auvergne was Lizzie. Lizzie was what was known as a Ta Ta or Wavy Paw lizard, an engaging little reptile which runs rapidly in short bursts, waving a front paw each time it stops for breath.

I first met Lizzie when I walked into my room one night after the evening meal and heard a very audible crunch on the floor beneath me. Groping for the light cord, (ever wary a cow's nose might be attached), I looked down at a small female Ta-Ta lizard. She had a very large cockroach in her mouth and she looked up at me curiously, her head cocked to one side. She had no fear of me and had probably been watching me for a long time while I had been unaware of her presence.

'If you're going to eat those disgusting things, you can live here as long as you like', I told her.

Lizzie became tame to the point where she would sleep the night on the cane chair, which doubled as my bedside table. I could reach out and stroke her gently along the tip of her tail, but that's all she would allow. She had the run of my room and I enjoyed her company.

A large male Ta Ta lizard arrived at the school door one day. I don't remember him asking me if he could date Lizzie, but my little friend's scaly belly had developed a roundness that told me she'd 'been to the pictures'[8] with her new friend. She disappeared out of my life forever very soon after, probably to raise her young away from my feet. I didn't think I would miss a lizard, but I certainly missed Lizzie and for many nights after, I would look at the cane chair in the hopes that she had come back.

Last, but not least of the Auvergne 'pets' was Norman! Part human and part animal, Norman was one of the jackaroos and I had the feeling he wanted to be one of my pets. 'Skirt'[9] was pretty scarce on some of these cattle stations and the blokes weren't all that choosy. About my height but built somewhat similar to a snake, Norman was pleasant enough and we would play some good games of cards with other staff members, especially when it was raining. However, try as he might, Norman just couldn't catch my eye. I've often wondered what became of him and I never saw him again after I left Auvergne.

---

8   A colloquial term for 'had sex with ...'
9   Females

Chapter 7

Ellenbrae Station

I don't remember how far through the year I had come as Auvergne's governess when my relationship with Camille appeared to sour. Long after I had left the station, I made excuses for some of her strange behaviour, thinking she was possibly suffering from menopause, but at the time I knew nothing about that physical condition and I've no doubt it was a pretty bad time for her. It certainly was for me.

I thought it had begun with young Mark, and perhaps it had. He had made himself particularly obnoxious to me one day in school and I regrettably lost my temper. Not being one to do this, tensions must have been growing between him and me for some time, until I finally yelled at him to remove himself from the classroom before I did. While I had a burning desire to do him some physical harm, I didn't touch him and he prudently disappeared before I changed

Chapter 7   Ellenbrae Station

my mind. When I walked out of the schoolroom a little later, I saw him duck inside the store where Camille was servicing the Aboriginal workers on 'store day'. I knew he would have told her about the event, his version no doubt, and I expected to be summoned to give an account from my perspective. That never eventuated, but a frosty silence descended between us. The atmosphere could have been sliced with a knife and at one of the weekly barbeques we had, Camille turned her back on all of us.

After enduring this for some time, I was longing to leave. However, I didn't feel I could up-stakes in the middle of the year, mostly for the children's sakes, so I remained on for as long as I could. I don't remember if I was able to finish the year's curriculum but I know I tried and I know how much harder each day became.

The family encouraged me to place an advertisement in the *Queensland Country Life* for another job and I followed that advice.

'Twenty-three-year-old girl seeks work on station ...' I wrote out for the advertisement, or words to that effect.

A week or two later, the mail plane arrived and we all congregated in the main house. Mail day only happened once a week if the airstrip was serviceable, so there were sometimes a couple of bags of mail and we always enjoyed this occasion. Mail Order catalogues were prized possessions and we would scan them from cover to cover.

Neville was the first to grab the *Queensland Country*

Life and disappeared behind its pages while we continued sorting mail. After a few minutes, we heard him chuckle. Then he began to laugh.

'Since when did you become a "gin"[10]?' he asked.

'Huh?' I responded, as I continued to place letters in their respective piles.

'Well, your advertisement reads "23-year-old gin seeking work ..."'

'Liar!' I laughed, punching his arm.

'Fair dinkum! If you don't believe me, take a look for yourself.' He handed me the paper and he wasn't pulling my leg.

I decided not to contact the *Country Life* to change the mistake, being curious to see what responses I might receive from it. I didn't have to wait long before two letters arrived.

The first came from a family in Queensland who fostered Aboriginal children and wanted me as a companion/ governess. Companion, maybe, but governess? No thank you, I thought.

The second was for the position of Jillaroo on Ellenbrae Station, about 129 km southwest of Wyndham. Not wanting to spend any more time on Auvergne, I settled for the second job and contacted Doug, Ellenbrae's manager. He informed me he would be in Kununurra the following week and asked me to meet him there for an interview.

Doug hired me, Aboriginal or not, and I accepted but

---

10   The colloquial term for an Aboriginal woman

Chapter 7 Ellenbrae Station

I didn't realise until I arrived on the station how little he had told me of what to expect. He obviously knew a soft white girl would never have accepted the position if he had, whereas an Aboriginal woman would have been much less likely to faint on seeing the conditions on offer.

I took my leave of Auvergne with a tiny pang of remorse and a whole truckload of relief. While I bore no resentment toward Camille for her coolness toward me, and probably contributed to the problem somehow, I had been increasingly miserable over the last half of my sojourn there. On the road to Kununurra to fly to Ellenbrae, I felt I had been suffocating for a long time and could suddenly breathe again. It was an extraordinary sensation.

It's quite possible my inability to cope with the problems at Auvergne were stress-related. Tino, the man I left Rhodesia to escape, had arrived back in my life again and the nauseous panic attacks I had suffered when I was going with him had returned! Because I hadn't been honest with him at the start, he was under the impression that I would soon be going home and that we would be married. My fibs had created a tangled web of deceit and I found myself telling more lies to try to extricate myself from this ghastly mess. My parents became involved because Tino wrote and told them I was coming home to marry him and even bought my air ticket, which he sent to them to forward to me. Not understanding why I hadn't told them, I can still remember the telegram from my father that was broadcast over Outback Radio for everyone to hear! It started 'Valerie, what the hell do you think you're doing ...?' In a mad panic, I quickly despatched a telegram back telling Mum and Dad not to worry and to return the air ticket to Tino with a note to say I would be writing to him. They complied, but they did worry. Mum told me later that Dad didn't sleep a wink for several weeks and I can't blame him! Fortunately, Tino made the final break easy for me. He resorted to blackmail.

Asserting to have a tape in his possession that he claimed would cause me a great deal of embarrassment, he informed me that if I were to meet someone else before a certain date and become engaged to them, he would send a copy of the tape to my parents, my future husband and his parents. He could easily accomplish this as he was also a private detective with worldwide contacts. At least he told me he was and I had no reason to doubt it. I even had experience with this shadowy aspect of his life when we were still together in Bulawayo and he contracted me to follow a woman one night, whose husband suspected she was conducting an affair. Sliding in and out of darkened doorways in the dead of night to avoid detection, I was paid well for my efforts but I quickly realised this wasn't something I was going to do again. I felt a right-royal hypocrite considering I was dating a married man myself and it could have been me in that poor woman's shoes!

Tino used to tell me that he would be able to track me down anywhere in the world and he would always know what I was doing. If I didn't believe him then, when he sent Graeme and me an engagement card long after his attempt to frighten me with his blackmail threat had failed, I did! No one had told him of our engagement, nor were there any engagement notices published anywhere in the world and it was then I became paranoid, distrusting even the radio personnel that manned the Flying Doctor base at Wyndham through which all our communication passed by radio transmitters. I was genuinely afraid they were 'Tino' contacts!

I had written to Tino and sarcastically thanked him for his gentlemanly attempt to persuade me to go back to him. I told him that if he did, indeed, have a tape in his possession, he could send it to whoever he liked and that I would sooner 'marry a Brahman bull' than hitch myself to a blackmailer. I never received a response to that letter and after the engagement card, he dropped right out of my life, apparently embarking on many adventures worldwide. He used to write long letters to my mother, detailing his voyages and exploits but that also discontinued when my parents returned to England. He was one more acquaintance who re-entered my life uninvited nearly thirty years later!

Doug's plane was a little one, but the trip to Ellenbrae was much easier than the trip to Auvergne. I had the front seat and some room to move. I also had an air vent that worked.

Ellenbrae Station was an education for me! There was only one building on the place, a prefab construction 3 m by 6 m divided into two rooms. One half was piled floor to ceiling with furniture and the other half contained desk, transmitter radio, fridge and saddlery. No sign anywhere of sleeping quarters. Doug hadn't told me there was no Mrs 'Doug' and now there appeared to be nowhere to sleep either. Apprehension intensified!

Doug finally directed me to my living quarters by throwing a casual gesture towards the bush.

'Just down there's where you'll camp,' he told me. 'Just down there' stood a four-cornered tent with a pole up the middle. One lonely piece of furniture was tucked in a corner — a cyclone netting stretcher, nothing more. Now I was really scared!

When Doug told me that he chose to throw his swag out next to the fire, I tried hard not to show my relief. It was probably in this short space of time that I felt most vulnerable. Ellenbrae couldn't be accessed by road at that time, except with enormous difficulty and the only viable way in or out was by plane. Doug was the pilot! Had he been a nasty type, I could be in hot water!

Whatever Doug's failings may have been, he was a rare personality. He was also a gentleman and never showed any inclination to want to molest me or make life difficult in that respect. There was no knowing if he would have been different had I been the 'gin' advertised in the *Queensland Country Life*. Many white men in the Northern Territory and Kimberley kept Aboriginal women by choice and the

Chapter 7 Ellenbrae Station

fact Doug went ahead and employed a white girl instead of waiting for the 'gin' he was expecting may have meant he needed assistance immediately and couldn't wait any longer.

My first evening at Ellenbrae was a surprise. Doug disappeared into the office for twenty minutes or so, leaving me to enjoy the magnificence of a typical northern sunset. I had just begun to wonder what had happened to him when he emerged with a plate of hors d'oeuvres he'd prepared, along with two containers of home-brewed beer, icy cold. He had quickly and emphatically informed me that I wouldn't have anything to do with the cooking, which suited me very well, and here he was looking like a waiter at the Ritz except for his clothing, complete with tea towel hung over his arm. At first, I thought this might have been put on as a kind of welcome, but this was an everyday ritual.

I actually grew to enjoy this stab at gentility in this remotest of locations very much. The sunsets, the flickering flames of the campfire, the sizzling of the evening meal in the frying pan, the plate of hors d'oeuvres and home-brewed beer were a wonderful mixture and the sounds of the Australian bush going to bed relaxed body and mind. When Doug had to go away for a day or two as he sometimes did, I would sit at the campfire alone and think of hors d'oeuvres and chilled home-brewed beer. I never dared to avail myself of these luxuries, so had to content myself with the fire, the sunset and my seriously 'rookie' cooking attempts.

A lot happened on my first day at Ellenbrae. Natural bodily functions provoked me into asking Doug where the toilet was. Having discovered my living quarters, I should have been suspicious and not held my hopes too high, but hope springs eternal, they say.

'Just grab that shovel and dig a hole over there,' I was directed. 'I want to eventually make a vegetable garden and we may as well start fertilising it now.'

Unfortunately for him, the veggie garden-to-be was immediately behind the hut, in full view of anyone who wanted to take a shower, so it was left to him to do the fertilising. I would 'go the extra mile' and walk into the bush whenever nature called.

That brings me to the shower! I had noticed a large Boab tree with a tap sticking out of it when we drove in. The tap was good for nothing more than an idiosyncrasy, but the shower was strategically placed behind the trunk of the tree in full view of anyone who wanted to 'fertilise the veggie garden'. It seemed we were doomed to keep an eye on each other at all times! A large slab of slate comprised the floor and there were no curtains or even a bush to afford a little privacy. A bucket of water and a gold-panning dish were the shower utensils. It was adequate, but I never felt comfortable when showering, and my eyes swivelled continuously from side to side throughout my ablutions, constantly on the lookout for peepers.

Only two intruders interrupted my bath time, one of which

Chapter 7 Ellenbrae Station

frightened ten years off my life. I heard a heavy footstep behind the tree and froze, ears pricked, tensed ready for flight. I've no idea where I would have flown to, clad only in my birthday suit. Suddenly, there was a loud snort and a very large, woolly-headed Hereford bull ambled up beside me. Doug had let him into the camp enclosure to 'mow the grass' but I was unaware of this. Eventually realising he wasn't out to do me any harm I completed my ablutions. At least he didn't stare at anything but the grass he was pursuing.

My second visitor in the 'bathroom' was a large frillyneck lizard. He parked himself on the trunk of a tree just above my head and remained motionless throughout my shower. He was quiet enough that I was able to softly stroke the end of his tail, which he seemed to enjoy. When I ventured further up, he considered I was being too bold and moved away. I never saw him again.

The wildlife at Ellenbrae was quite tame. I suppose they hadn't been hunted by anyone, and Doug certainly encouraged them. While we ate our evening meals beside the campfire each evening, a couple of sand goannas would cautiously approach and gratefully swallow any offerings we threw their way. Vast numbers of blood finches also inhabited the area and they would sometimes hop onto one's boot while one was engaged in conversation. They were stunningly beautiful in their flocks, making me think of torrents of rubies when they flew en masse into the bushes.

It was a rather lonely life at Ellenbrae. Doug wasn't a

talkative person and was quite often away. My social life revolved around a fencing crew consisting of two white men and one Aboriginal woman, and Les, the horse breaker later on. Up to this time, I hadn't had a lot to do with the Aboriginal people and as luck would have it, the fencers' lady decided her man was eying me off. I didn't have the faintest idea she felt this way because I had no proof that her fellow was watching me. It all came to a head when she wobbled out of the bushes to the campfire one evening where Doug, the two fencers and I sat. She'd given the alcohol a pretty good nudge, but thankfully she was protective towards me and abusive towards her partner.

'You no-good b ...' she shouted. 'I gotta look after dis poor liddle gel. She bin come properly long way from her home 'n she got no mummy lookin' after her. You can't be lookin' at her dat'ay (that way).' Abruptly, she sat down and dragged me onto her lap with reptilian speed.

'I bin look after you, Val' she slurred, patting me happily. 'I nebber let him get you.' I was fairly sure he wouldn't get me, but probably not for the same reason she had in mind. He just wasn't my type at all.

Until the fencers came, Ellenbrae had been in drought conditions. The river was completely dry and Doug would send me on horseback down the river each day to find the soaks so we would know where the cattle watered, or could be watered. The heat was in the high thirties and I very nearly perished on one of these excursions.

Never a big water drinker I left on my daily trip one day without having a decent drink. I was green to the harsh reality of this dry continent, but I learned my lesson well. I began to get thirsty towards midday and by midafternoon when I returned home, I broke all the First Aid rules I'd learned for people who were perishing. I drank until my stomach couldn't hold any more. Within minutes, I was paralysed with pain and spent the rest of the afternoon on my bed curled into a rigid ball hoping to recover really fast or die really quickly. I didn't die, but nothing could have persuaded me at the time that survival was the preferable option.

When the rains came, they came with a fearsome storm sometime in the middle of the night. Gale-force wind howled while heavy rain thundered on the canvas of my tent and I lay on my cyclone stretcher with one foot jammed against the centre pole in the hope that I could prevent the entire tent from flying away. Badly frightened, I found myself cramping with the effort. Then, as suddenly as it had started, the storm stopped and I spent the rest of the night in a wet swag. When I emerged from my battered abode the following morning, I looked out at the devastation. The heads of trees that had been blown down in the storm had landed only a metre or so from my tent and I was made aware in no uncertain terms that I could have died that night.

Campbell Creek, which ran past the camp flooded due to a heavy downfall on a property upstream. It wasn't even trickling when I started out on horseback that morning, so I crossed over to check a paddock on the other side. I had left some of the horses shut in the yard to be moved to another paddock on my return, but by the time I reached the river on the homeward trail, it was running 'a banker'[11]. It was now some sixty to ninety metres wide, a raging, frothing torrent that swept and tossed logs and debris effortlessly before it. Knowing nothing of these 'flash' floods, I worried about the horses left shut in the yard. They'd die if I didn't somehow get over and let them out, I thought. I know now that even if the river had stayed up for a week, it's improbable the horses would have been worse off than perhaps a little hungry. They had access to water and plenty of body condition to keep them going for quite a while.

Not knowing this and in a panic, I decided I would have to swim this river. I had read books that told me I should walk upstream before entering the water, as the swiftness of the current would carry me away. I thought it more sensible to walk upstream first and hopefully arrive close to the place I wanted to go than to have to walk a long way back after an exhausting swim. Tying my horse at the departure point, I glanced furtively around to ensure no one was watching, then stripped down to my underwear and dived in. I was actually amazed at how easy it was and I landed effortlessly on the other side, right at the campsite.

---

11   From bank to bank wide

Chapter 7 Ellenbrae Station

It was only years later I realised the danger of being struck on the head by a tree trunk without knowing it was there and I learned that people had drowned for that reason. I was lucky and succeeded in my mission, getting back to my horse without difficulty.

I had noticed the fencing gang with their fleet of equipment had been stopped by the torrent also. I wandered down to where they were, feeling very proud of myself and sat with them to wait for the flood water to recede. Taking longer than I thought it should impatience finally got the better of me apart from running out of things to talk about, and I crossed the river on horseback without trouble. It was still too deep for the vehicles and the grader eventually had to tow them across.

Christmas Day was closing in when Les, the horse breaker, arrived. I was glad of his company as Doug left the station over the Christmas period, the fencing crew had completed their job and moved on and it was the first time I had spent Christmas away from my family.

Les and I got on very well. He was a shortish man with grey hair, bandy legs and a lively sense of humour. I don't know how old he was, but I reckoned he was around fifty. He would break the young horses into the saddle, and then he and I would ride them out together to round off their education. My horse would always be one of the old horses so the youngsters would have a steady role model to follow and Les and I had a lot of fun on these little jaunts. His

*Horse breaker Les at Ellenbrae station
next to the Boab with the tap.*

keen sense of humour would have my sides splitting and I became very fond of him.

Christmas Day was quite different to anything I was accustomed to. No presents under the tree, or Christmas stockings bulging with bits and pieces for me this year. I don't think Santa had a snowball's chance in Marble Bar[12] of finding me! Les broke in horses, we rode together and

---

12 Marble Bar was founded in 1893 & has the reputation of being Australia's hottest town with 38C temperatures for days on end.

yarned over a cup of tea and a corned beef sandwich for Christmas lunch but it was still a good day.

There was some pressure building between Doug and myself after seven weeks in his employ. That may not sound very long but I was told on multiple occasions later that to stay seven weeks on Ellenbrae was a record! I think I must have been getting short tempered because whenever we mustered cattle, Doug always made me chase the cranky[13] scrubbers that made a break for freedom while he plodded along behind the rest of the quiet cattle, scarcely having to raise a trot, and certainly never a sweat. I didn't mind doing this, but I thought it would be nice if he took the responsibility once in a while.

On one of these occasions, I was chasing a mad horned mickey[14] through the bush in a concerted effort to wheel him back to the mob. He headed straight towards the river with me blowing down his back when he suddenly disappeared from sight. It was too late to apply the brakes and horse and I sailed out into open space. The riverbank had appeared without warning and dropped a sharp three and a half metres into the sandy bed below. Fortunately, the horse kept his feet and neither of us was hurt. Nor was the mickey, whose puny backside I watched vanishing into the bushes on the far side while the horse and I caught our breath. It was this incident that startled my feelings

---

13 Short-tempered, angry, cross.
14 Young wild bull, usually with long, sharp horns!

of discontent into wakefulness. The day that brought the whole show down a short time after the mickey escaped wasn't without its funny side.

Doug, Les and I were drafting[15] the horses when Doug asked me to do something with the gate. Not the clearest of speakers at any time, I couldn't catch the drift of his mumblings and asked him to repeat his message. Still not able to hear him, I tried to figure it out for myself and of course I did the opposite of what he wanted me to do. He abused me roundly and I spat the dummy[16].

'If you'd only open your stupid mouth and speak clearly, I'd have heard what you said. Do the job yourself,' I snarled at him. I stalked off, trying my best to look cool, calm and collected. I might have managed it too had I not tripped on a rock and landed spraddle-legged to prevent myself from falling face down. Doug eventually caught up with me at the campfire where I sat gazing glassy-eyed into its flames.

'I really don't think you're suited to this job,' he said bluntly. I wanted to tell him it was him I wasn't suited to but I bit my tongue.

'You're quite right,' I agreed and once again, I was fired and resigned simultaneously.

---

15 Separating horses or cattle into different pens or paddocks.
16 To lose one's temper.

Chapter 8

Nicholson Station

Doug flew me to Kununurra and I eventually finished up outside the post office, sitting on my swag and having no idea what I was going to do next. I had seldom visited Kununurra when I worked at Auvergne, so I didn't know anyone and hence had no one I felt comfortable turning to. I squatted there in contemplation, prepared to camp outside the post office, which I figured would probably be the safest place apart from a motel, which I couldn't afford.

I was surprised out of my reverie by someone shouting my name from a passing car. The vehicle parked and the Newry station manager's wife, Gail, stepped out. Newry belonged to the same company that owned Auvergne and they shared a common boundary, so I had come to know these people reasonably well.

'What are you doing here?' Gail inquired. When I told her I was jobless and homeless, she took charge.

'I'm just off to see the Hacketts,' she said. 'Come along with me and they may know somewhere you can go or have heard of a job somewhere.' Grateful to get away from the public eye for a while, I loaded my gear into the back of Gail's car.

The Hacketts turned out to be a large family. I think there were five children, perhaps six. When Mrs Hackett heard of my situation, she promptly invited me to stay. She would talk to Jim the Stock and Station Agent, and ask him to find a job for me, since that was one of his commissions. I had never heard of a Stock and Station Agent before that time.

Jim turned up on the Hackett's doorstep that same night. He had found a domestic position at Nicholson Station, but no one would be coming to town for a week, so I'd have to wait until then. I think Mrs Hackett may have been quite pleased as I was able to help with the children and was happy to do so to repay them for their kindness to me.

While at the Hacketts, I had what could have been, and actually was, a very embarrassing experience! There was a ball being held in the town so I dressed up in a long evening dress I'd ordered through the mail order catalogue while at Auvergne and went along. Amongst the many new friends that I made that night was Jim, a tall, good-looking fellow from Swaziland in Africa, now called Eswatini. Still being a

Chapter 8 Nicholson Station

little homesick for my country, I was delighted to find him and he seemed pretty happy to meet me too. I've discovered over the years that ex Rhodesians and South Africans seem to feel quite a strong bond towards one another. To his shame because I didn't know she existed, Jim forgot about his girlfriend in our mutual passion for Africa and our memories of it and when it was time for me to go home, he offered me a lift.

The Hacketts had a swimming pool in their yard, one of those above ground aluminium contraptions. It was empty except for two or three inches of water in the bottom. Jim and I settled ourselves against the side of the pool, still talking and reminiscing when the side of the pool suddenly caved in. We both landed on our backs with our legs in the air and it's difficult to describe how tricky it is to get oneself out of such a predicament when clad in a long ball gown! During our efforts to extricate ourselves, I couldn't help wondering how this must look to anyone who might just be passing by. I had to hope that if there was someone out there, they were just staggering home from a drinking binge and thought they had the DTs!

That broke our little party up and I went to bed for what was left of the night, only to lie awake most of the time wondering how I could explain to the Hacketts that a rogue elephant hadn't sidled up to their pool in the middle of the night

Loud banging out in the yard woke me earlier than I

wished and I found Jim diligently repairing the pool. He did a very good job and there were no tell-tale signs of the midnight drama. I didn't ask him what he'd told the Hacketts. As for Jim and his girl, I never saw him again but I did see his girlfriend years later. She had married someone else and had children and she remembered very kindly the night I 'stole' Jim from her. I'm glad she didn't remember it quite as well as I did!

At the end of my week with the Hacketts, a young jackaroo named Fred from Spring Creek Station arrived in town and I was to travel back to Spring Creek with him. Spring Creek was an outstation of Nicholson Station and the Nicholson overseer was organised to take me the rest of the journey to Nicholson. I never saw the Hackett family again either, but will always remember them with gratitude for their hospitality to a total stranger when I had never felt more alone and exposed.

Len came to fetch me from Spring Creek and he featured quite a bit in my life, on and off. He was a short man with the usual bandy legs I'd come to expect of blokes on cattle stations, enormous droopy brown eyes and dark, curly hair. A large hook of a nose was parked above his top lip, which occasionally sported a luxuriant moustache which fell over the sides of the mouth. Wearing a sombrero, spurs and a colourful cape, he could have been cast as Speedy Gonzales in a Warner Brothers movie. Ironically, Len was nicknamed 'The Desert Rat'.

Chapter 8 Nicholson Station

All the way to Nicholson, Len described the head stockman to me with some colourful language sprinkled here and there. He portrayed him as arrogant and 'a bit full of himself' and by the time we arrived at our destination I was prepared to meet an unattractive, conceited narcissist. What strode into the dining room the next morning was far from unattractive and a glaring contrast to the Desert Rat! Standing at around 180 cm, he was clad in jeans and a shirt with the sleeves cut out, displaying tanned muscular arms. He carried himself erect with a notable swagger and narcissist or not, I thought the Nicholson Head Stockman was at least very pleasant to look at. Alison, a nice English girl with whom I was to share living quarters introduced me to the head stockman the following morning at breakfast.

'Graeme, this is Val. She's the new domestic and she loves horse riding.' Graeme sat down opposite us with his heaped plate. After liberally sprinkling salt on his breakfast, the man looked me straight in the eye and spoke. No 'How do you do?' or 'G'day, pleased to meet you.' Nothing quite that genteel.

'I won't allow women in my stock camp,' he stated flatly.

I have to admit I was taken aback by this and rendered speechless for a second or two. I hadn't even considered being in his stock camp and all the things Len had told me about this person echoed in my ears. Arrogant, full of himself, probably spoilt rotten, the thoughts tumbled through my head. Finding my tongue which I think was

Nicholson head stockman Graeme with his dog Caesar.

hiding halfway down my throat, I looked straight back at the 'hunk'.

'I wouldn't want to be in your stock camp,' I retorted before I began eating my cooling breakfast.

I don't remember how our friendship began but friendships are limited on remote cattle properties and one is surrounded by the same people for an entire year if they don't up-stakes and pull out in the middle of the mustering season. Graeme worked away from the station most of the time with the stockmen, bringing my circle of 'friends' down to mostly women: domestics, the bookkeeper and the manager's wife. When the stock camp returned to the homestead, the men broke in young horses and I spent my spare time watching. I hadn't seen Les break the horses in at Ellenbrae, and the procedure fascinated me. I suppose I got to know Graeme better by doing this and he began to relax a little around me when he figured I wasn't going to beg him to let me spend a day in the stock camp. I continued to be wary of him though.

It wasn't very long after that I found Alison crying on her bed and discovered she had a crush on the head stockman. Having low self-esteem at this stage in my life, I remember asking her what I had done to make her so upset. She told me that she had been trying to attract Graeme's attention for months and then I had just come along and snitched him out from under her nose with little apparent effort. How could I do such a thing? I was mortified! I had no idea she was even remotely interested in Graeme and I certainly wasn't aware that I was 'flirting' or sending out 'available' signals. On the contrary, I thought I was being appropriately cool towards him, given the quality of the welcome I received when I arrived. She had to be kidding or she knew something I didn't.

Alison left shortly after this event and was replaced by a willowy American girl with long dark hair. Her name was Marion and she and I got along well together. I taught her how to ride and Graeme would leave horses in the yard for us if I asked him to. In one instance, he forgot to leave a horse in for Marion so I walked several kilometres into the paddock to catch one for her. This was no effort to me because I enjoyed having her company. Besides, I guess it gave my low self-image a boost to be better at doing something than someone else and to be in a position where I could be the instructor.

Marion hadn't been with us all that long when I noticed a distinctive cooling of the atmosphere between her and the manager's wife, Robyn. Marion had become unusually surly over a period of time and one day, she hitched a ride on a truck that was passing through the station in order to get away for the weekend. She apparently didn't tell anyone she was going and unfortunately for her it rained heavily while she was gone, preventing her from resuming work on the Monday. She was absent for a week and when she finally was able to return, Robyn chose to dock[17] a week's wage from her pay packet for not having contacted the station to tell them what had happened.

I don't think it was long after that when I made a *big* mistake. Robyn asked me in conversation if I thought Marion was happy at Nicholson. Marion was quite obviously not happy and had been showing it for some time so I answered the question truthfully and thought no more about it.

At breakfast one Saturday morning, I detected a sub-zero chill in the air when Marion walked into the dining room. She scowled at me across the floor and all through breakfast, she made slicing comments directed straight at me without actually talking to me. I was confused and had no idea what had brought about this venomous behaviour. No amount

---

17 Deduct from a wage

Chapter 8 Nicholson Station

of brain-racking came up with a reasonable solution so I finally plucked up the courage to ask.

'Marion, what's chewing at you? If you have a problem with me, perhaps you should just tell me what it is.' If looks were daggers, I'd have haemorrhaged to death on the dining room floor.

'Did you tell Robyn I wasn't happy here?' she glared across the table. There it was! This tiny shred of gossip had come back to bite me on the bum. When I tried to justify myself by telling her I had only answered my boss's question truthfully, it was like talking to a wall.

'It's none of your business whether I am or not.' Her voice cracked and she seemed close to breaking. 'You had no right to tell Robyn I wasn't and now I've lost my job because of you!' This was news to me. I hadn't known Robyn had sacked her and I did feel some degree of guilt. Annoyance also over the fact that she was being punished twice for one misdemeanour. That feeling quickly dissipated however, when the cook passed on another piece of gossip that cut me to ribbons and upset me for at least twelve months after!

'Marion told me she'd always hated you, but she didn't say anything because you wouldn't have taught her how to ride if she had,' Cookie told me conversationally at lunch like it was no big deal. I couldn't believe how much that stung, and for many months I would think about it. Sometimes, it would niggle at me while I was sweeping rooms and my sweeping actions became increasingly agitated the longer

I dwelt on it. I suspect I stirred up the dust rather than actually removing it during these sessions and I can laugh at it now, but the hurt that one remark caused me was a lesson for me. If I ever hate someone that much, I'll either tell them or shut up!

I later figured that Marion was probably also in love with the head stockman as Alison had been. Who on earth wasn't? The fact that a relationship had been growing between him and me had possibly been somewhere at the root of the problem. It seemed there were plenty of women who would have liked to drop a rope on the lad and when we were eventually engaged, I had to write letters to two of them to tell them he was 'no longer available' and get him to sign them! How embarrassing!

My task at Nicholson was to clean out the men's quarters and keep their rooms tidy. Not such a bad job, but there was one building I dreaded doing each day. An old pensioner named Bob inhabited it and it seemed his only goal in life was to either drink or smoke himself to death. He was a nice old bloke but when I had to face his quarters in the morning, I remember thinking that if death was what he was searching for, he would hopefully find it fast! What a revolting mess! Part of the problem was his floor. Not made of nice smooth cement like the rest of the men's quarters, this was comprised of slabs of limestone that could be found in great quantities by the rivers and was used to floor bough sheds, meat houses and outside barbeque areas etc.

Chapter 8 Nicholson Station

It should *never* have been used on the floors of alcoholic smokers' quarters! It was lovely to look at, being heavily pockmarked by the wear of water cascading across it for centuries one supposes, but what a terrible floor to sweep and keep clean! Old Bob used the pockmarks as ashtrays and the more sozzled he became, the more likely it was that he would spill beer on the floor. Such spills would meander until they combined with the cigarette butts and ashes and made a glorious concoction that sent my olfactory nerves into shock and my stomach into 'clench' mode! The only way of coping with this revolting situation was to bring in the hose and sluice the filth out with copious amounts of water. Even then, the smell still lingered, either in the air or trapped in my nostril hairs!

When I first started my job at Nicholson, I was given a choice of either the laundress position or cleaning out the men's quarters. In hindsight, I probably should have chosen the laundry but then my education into the habits of drunks wouldn't have been so well rounded. I was glad Marion was given the laundress position because if it had been I that shrunk the man-sized woollen sweater into a child-sized woollen sweater, my low self-image would surely have never recovered!

CHAPTER 9

The bush romance

While I was packing my bags to come to Australia, my mother approached me with a piece of paper in her hand.

'What's that?' I asked. Mum told me it was my birth certificate and perhaps I should take it with me.

'Whatever for? I know when I was born, don't I?' Mum explained patiently that I might need it for all sorts of things, or want to get married to someone in Australia. I was appalled at that suggestion! In the process of running away from Tino after enduring two of the most miserable years of my young life, I had no intention of getting involved with anyone else, especially not on what was to be only a twelve-month trip. Mother's wisdom won the toss and I laid the certificate on the bottom of my suitcase, fully expecting it would remain there until I returned to Rhodesia.

Chapter 9 The bush romance

During my week in Kununurra with the Hacketts, I was re-acquainted with Centurion's owner, Lloyd's brother George. He was recovering from a drinking binge and had allegedly taken a bite out of the side of his glass, crunched it up and swallowed it. I'll never know if this was a mental illness or he simply was intoxicated enough to mistake his glass for party food. It was rumoured this was a fairly common practice with George and I would almost sweat bullets thinking of the agony he must have endured while excreting! My twisted sense of humour also allowed me a sly grin when I imagined the possibly associated hazard of passing wind!

The Hacketts, in their usual hospitable way had taken George in and nursed him over his ordeal. I sometimes took meals to him. On one of these occasions, I mentioned that I had landed a job on Nicholson Station.

'There's a good-looking young head stockman there,' George confided. 'You'll end up marrying him.' No ifs or buts, he spoke with prophetic authority on this matter. When finally confronted by this 'good looking young head stockman' who didn't want women in his stock camp, I decided old George had placed his bet on the wrong horse. There wasn't any way I'd be marrying this bloke!

I suppose stranger things have happened, but as the weeks passed and I sometimes rode out with the stockmen on weekends for pleasure, Graeme and I finally became friends. He had a blue heeler-cross dog named Caesar and I loved him. In fact, everyone on the station loved Caesar. Graeme wasn't in favour of anyone touching his dog as this is supposed to ruin working dogs, but he didn't prevent me from playing with Caesar when opportunity arose. Tragically, it was Caesar that revealed his 'chauvinist' master's deeply disguised tender streak.

We had ridden out one day and Caesar accompanied us as he always did. A few hours later, when I bent to pat him, he flinched and alarm bells began to ring. This was characteristic of a dog that had taken strychnine bait. I told Graeme and it seemed the whole station came out to save Caesar. We poured salt down his throat and someone swung him around by the back legs in an attempt to make him vomit. Always sweet-tempered and cooperative, Caesar deposited the contents of his stomach on the lawn and we all breathed a sigh of relief. We all hoped it was enough.

The following evening, I went to Graeme's quarters to see him and find out how his dog was faring. Caesar had seemingly settled down on his bed in the veranda after the 'doing' we had given him. He'd had a drink of water and things were looking hopeful. This evening, as I was talking to Graeme, I noticed an abnormal stillness in the dog. I watched him closely while we chatted until I was certain.

'Graeme,' I said as calmly as I could, 'I think Caesar's dead.'

'No, he's OK,' Graeme assured me. 'He's been pretty good today.'

Chapter 9   The bush romance

'I think you should check him,' I continued. 'He's lying awfully still.'

Caesar was dead and I stood helplessly by as a young man's heart broke, the narcissist I had thought to be cold and arrogant.

My feelings towards Graeme changed at this point. It also seemed to be around this time when he folded up the macho image that he'd wrapped himself in and put it away. He let down his guard and there was no further need to hold up the wall he'd built around himself. I felt a strong bond developing between me and the kind and funny human being that emerged.

When I was in my teens, Dad always said that the man I married should put his livestock first and his wife second in order of priority. I discovered that Graeme fitted the bill perfectly in this regard and Dad would have smiled with satisfaction if he had ridden out with us one weekend.

Graeme had delegated a horse to me during my time at Nicholson. Her name was Dolly and she wasn't a pretty horse. Part draught horse, part wild donkey I reckoned, she had a head like a hairy beef bucket[18] with a slightly Roman nose and a pair of piggy eyes that twinkled in her common head. A pair of whiskery ears perched on top like antenna and an over-relaxed bottom lip flopped in time with her feet when she moved. Her hooves were mostly covered by hair in all seasons, but especially in

---

18   Twenty litre drum used to boil corned beef in at the Stock camps

the winter. What Dolly lacked in equine magnificence, she made up for in personality. We were ideally suited.

On occasions when we used to go mustering, Dolly and I would take our position at the back of the mob to push the cattle along. I didn't have to do anything. Dolly would walk from side to side on her own initiative but what amused me most was her chosen method of encouraging cattle to move a bit faster. If an adult animal lagged behind long enough to tick her off, Dolly would sink her long yellow teeth into the animal's tail, but if young calves fell behind, she would

My goofy pal, Dolly, Nicholson station.

Chapter 9 The bush romance

gently nudge them along. I never saw her bite a calf, and I never saw her just nudge an adult animal.

One afternoon, we gathered on the edge of a narrow stream, preparing to cross. Graeme led the way, his horse taking a powerful leap to the other side without getting its feet wet. Dolly was to follow next. Teetering precariously on the bank, she shuffled her feet with trepidation. After thirty seconds or so of serious deliberation, she bunched her hindquarters beneath her and bounded off the bank with the grace of a pregnant hippo. Being of smaller stature with shorter legs than most other station horses, Dolly landed in the middle of the creek. Her head bogged down in the mud between her front legs and she toppled helplessly onto her side with me still in the saddle. Now here was a dilemma! I couldn't move until Dolly regained her feet, so I was able to leisurely survey the activities on the opposite bank while she made up her mind what she should do. Graeme had airlifted himself out of the saddle and was ripping his shirt off, presumably either to wade in and rescue me or at least to wipe the mud off my face so I could see where I was going. How naive of me!

Dolly eventually clambered clumsily to her hairy feet and waded towards Graeme, her eyes and face caked with quickly crusting mud. I slowly stood up, expecting my knight in shining armour to rush to my side but nothing happened. Wiping the mud out of my own eyes, I looked up to see Dolly being lovingly tended by my shirtless head stockman friend while I floundered in the creek, taking care of myself. I could almost hear my dad applauding somewhere in the distance.

'Well, she couldn't do it herself, could she?' Graeme explained when we recounted the story many times in later years, and of course he was right.

None of the stations had television when we worked in the Kimberly. Our entertainment came in the form of a movie once every month and each station owned a film projector. A screen was set up at the end of the driveway in front of the manager's house or on the workshop wall at Nicholson and all the station personnel would carry a chair or blanket out and sit under the stars to enjoy the show.

On other nights, we would usually gang together in one of the quarters with a few bottles of beer, turn the music up and simply socialise. Occasionally, we would take quite long walks out on to the plain and it was here I learned about Orion the Hunter and the Seven Sisters. I was never much good at picking out the star constellations, preferring to just enjoy their incredible beauty and my awe at the wonders of the southern sky may have played a part in my eventual search for the spiritual nourishment I had been lacking.

Sometimes on these nightly walks, we would see what looked like a flickering torchlight way out on the plains at one of the stock camps where, so the story for gullible young foreigners goes, a Chinese camp cook died and was buried. It was his ghost. I don't think I believed the story but the fact remains — no one was camped out there on the nights we saw the light and yet it was definitely a moving light. We decided it had to be a min min[19] light but, by all accounts I ever heard about these inexplicable light sources, this one didn't behave in the traditional min min manner. It looked exactly as if someone was walking with a torch.

As we became more familiar with one another, I learned much about Graeme's family back home in Kingaroy, Queensland. Third eldest of a family of six boys and one girl, he grew up thinking for many years that he must have been adopted. Part of the reason for this was that, having had three boys, his mother gave birth to her only daughter when Graeme was just sixteen months old. It was somewhat natural that he was shelved and left mostly to his own devices at a time when he needed to be allowed to be a baby and this sat hard on his shoulders for some time. However, he did have a wonderful relationship with both his sister and his maternal grandmother. One who could outwork most men, Nanna McLennan would put three children on the back of the old horse in front and behind her and gallop off down the paddock to get the cows home for milking. It was evident Graeme adored her and it was the second time I witnessed emotion when he spoke of her death not very long before he went north.

There were occasions when the stockmen would hurt

---

19 A light phenomenon that has often been reported in outback Australia (Wikipedia)

themselves in the course of their duties and on one such instance, horses had trodden on Graeme and jackaroo Neil's toes. They both lost their toenails but in the process of doing so, they would hobble to my cabin each night after tea and I'd bathe and bandage their feet for them. Nursing skills on stations were carried out with the help of the Flying Doctor chest, full of various medications all given their own number. In the event of something serious one could contact the Flying Doctor on the radio, describe the symptoms and the doctor would prescribe a number and give the dosage details. It was a wonderfully simple system and often we had to administer injections and medication to various patients.

One such event occurred when Daphne the bookkeeper, also a Rhodesian, and I developed conditions that required penicillin injections. Because the manager Len and his wife Robyn were away on holidays, the task automatically passed on to the head stockman. Daphne, the fifty plus year old bookkeeper assured me that the buttock was the best place to receive an injection, but being shy and not in love with the thought of exposing my backside to the man I was becoming emotionally attached to, I rolled up my sleeve and took my shot in the arm. Not Daphne, though. Asking Graeme to wait, she vanished into her room for a few seconds, and then called out. The shock of seeing her white bum turned towards the ceiling was almost more than he could handle and we were amazed he was able to complete the task with a dead-pan expression!

Chapter 9 The bush romance

It didn't seem long before I was finally allowed entrance to the stock camp and those were wonderful days for me. My childhood dream fulfilled, I spent as many weekends as I could camping out under the stars, mustering cattle from dawn to dark, or branding, dehorning and castrating cattle already mustered. The choking dust and saddle-weary backside my childhood dream hadn't included were of little consequence to me. Robyn told me many years later that I spent a lot of time in the station yards when the men were home, and that if she was unable to find me, she knew where to look. I don't remember that and I suppose it proves that one needs to behave properly throughout life because you never know who is missing you, or watching your behaviour!

It was during my time on Nicholson that I subscribed to a magazine that looked very much like the *Time* magazine. I craved news, but *Time* was heavy going for me and I didn't want to waste my money on a magazine that wouldn't be properly read. *Plain Truth* seemed to have articles to which I could relate, articles that appeared to hold promise for an answer to some of the questions of life that had bothered me. For many years I had suffered from low self-esteem and I developed the eating disorder bulimia whereby one gorges food and then forcibly throws it all up again. I smoked and behaved badly at social gatherings, often being heralded as 'the life of the party' because of the smutty jokes I told, and while I never actually disgraced myself (or I don't remember if I did) I had drunk far too much far too often. This gave me the courage I didn't have of my own accord but it was beginning to dawn on me that my tactics to gain acceptance weren't working. If someone was livelier than me at a party, or told a cruder joke than I did, people's attention would quickly drift away from me and gravitate toward them and so I would try harder to win them back, heaping one bad mistake on another. Now, out in the middle of the Australian outback surrounded by quietness and not much else to do but contemplate, I had embarked on a soul-searching journey.

Because of the influence of the Catholic school that I attended in South Africa, I had packed a pocket New Testament in my bags when I left home. It remained unpacked in my case until now and I found myself reading the Gospels and marvelling at this man Jesus. Whether an historical or mythological figure I had no idea, but his personality attracted me like a magnet. I found myself yearning to be like him and to have the same strengths that he portrayed and so began my prayer life. The only prayer I had ever prayed was The Lord's Prayer, which we had been forced to learn by heart from early childhood, and I had no idea I could talk to God as I would to any friend so The Lord's Prayer took a hiding!

My first *Plain Truth* magazine startled me! It was a religious publication, put out by the Worldwide Church of God. This wasn't what I had wanted, but I read it anyway

Chapter 9 The bush romance

and was astonished. The articles spoke of all the things that had hurt or bothered me throughout my life but to add weight to what they were saying, they would point to scriptures from the New Testament. I looked these up and the unfolding wisdom I was beginning to see was amplified every day. It was here I learned, and eventually believed, that I was made up of two bodies — a physical figure and a spiritual essence or 'inner man' and it was here at Nicholson that my 'double life' began.

CHAPTER 10

The bush engagement

In the months that followed, many new experiences came my way. While I had developed a sort of a faith in God, He still didn't take up too much of my time and I figured as so many do that as long as I tried to be nice to people and was 'a good person' God would find me acceptable.

My friendship with Graeme had grown to a different dimension and I was questioning whether this was 'love'. I remembered asking my mother when I was still quite young how one could know they had met the right person to marry.

'You'll know dear,' she assured me. 'It's a bit hard to define but you'll miss not having them around and always be looking forward to their return.'

In hindsight, this was probably a more adequate answer than I thought it was back then. Even if tensions between us can become a bit tight at times, there's always a deep sense

Chapter 10   The bush engagement

of loneliness when Graeme has to go away for any length of time and I eagerly look forward to his homecoming.

I'm sure there were other criteria that indicated to me something was going on, but the sadness I felt when the stock camp headed out and I knew I might not see my 'mate' for ten days or so was what I remember most. I also vividly recall the feelings that came with every cloud of dust on the road and the excited anticipation that perhaps it was Graeme coming to get some necessary equipment from the station. I had been brought up in such a way that I would never dare speak my feelings to him, so I kept them under my hat and life progressed in easy camaraderie.

We had travelled to attend the Renner Springs Picnic Races and Rodeo on the Barkly Tablelands approximately 1,000 km away when Graeme asked me to marry him. Still battling with a low self-image, I remember my response so clearly.

'I'm not a very nice person to live with.' I can't remember how he replied to that but he obviously thought he knew me well enough to think I was making much ado about nothing so we announced our engagement sometime later on our way home from a party on Sturt Creek Station. We had stopped to open a gate in the middle of the flattest stretch of downs country I'd ever seen and pulled aside to let Len and Robyn, who were travelling behind us, pass through. They stopped to offer us a drink of water and while we were partaking, other vehicles drew up and stopped. We figured that was as good a time as any to tell them our news and it passed through the convoy within seconds under the mercilessly hot Kimberly sun.

Len and Robyn weren't actually the first to know. We had confided in one of our jackaroos early that morning and I can still remember his joyful antics. I never did ask him why such a reaction but thought it might have been due to a hangover from the previous evening's activities and the fact he'd probably dosed himself on a bit of 'the hair of the dog' [20] that bit him.

We purchased my engagement ring by mail order, a sapphire with two small diamonds either side. I was very proud of it and wore it happily. Fortunately, one didn't have to wear pantihose much on stations as the ring was a little too high-set for my liking but the flattest on offer. I also retrieved my birth certificate from the bottom of my suitcase and appreciated my mother's wisdom in persuading me to take it with me!

Nicholson Station had two dining rooms. Tradition had it that the manager, his wife, the head stockman, jackaroos, bookkeepers and mechanics all ate in what we lower mortals called the 'posh' dining room. There, the white linen was laid out with spotless cutlery and one didn't dare to enter that sacred place with unwashed hands, or ears for that matter. The chosen ones were carefully scrutinised by

---

20 Another beer or alcoholic drink, which had the very temporary effect of making one feel a bit better.

Chapter 10 The bush engagement

the eagle-eye of ex hospital Matron, Robyn before seating. The rest of us domestics, cook, grader driver, fencers and hangers-on all ate in the dining room that was attached to the kitchen. Not for us the white linen and finery but none of us complained and we all got on well together.

When Graeme and I publicised our engagement, I expected that things might change and I would be called up to the higher realms. Not so, or at least not for quite some time so we continued to eat in our separate dining rooms until Robyn, considering what I'm sure was merely an oversight, invited me to the 'posh' dining room with profuse apologies. I don't remember getting to enjoy it for long as Graeme and I were sent to Flora Valley Station next door to caretake while the manager took his annual leave. Still, I had been recognised as the prospective wife of the head stockman and in some ways, it was like a homecoming.

What was to be only a three or four-week stay at Flora Valley turned into a four-month stint. The manager was accused of cattle duffing[21] and was given notice to leave so we had to fill in until a new manager could be arranged. It was the 'Wet', and wet it was! The 72 km or so to Nicholson took two hours to cover in a Toyota four-wheel drive, most of it sideways, and the black soil plains on which Flora Valley homestead stood became a trap that held the station truck in its sticky grip for over four months before anyone could get

---

21 Stealing cattle

out to rescue it. That gave the ants sufficient time to build their nest throughout the cabin.

It was while at Flora Valley that we heard on the Kimberly grape vine there was a Justice of the Peace, or a marriage celebrant who would marry people by mail. Thinking we would never leave Flora Valley again, and realising that our living arrangements were not 'right' according to the morals we had both inherited, we set about making plans to 'wed by mail'. It was a simple matter of sending the appropriate paperwork back and forth until they had all been signed and witnessed by the appropriate people and there it was — one was married. Unfortunately, while everything else was getting stuck, our plan came unstuck. The JP was away on holidays. I was sorry about that because not only did I want to be married but I also rather fancied the idea of being different, and to be married by mail would certainly have been that.

After languishing at Flora Valley for four of the wettest months I think I'd ever known to that point, we were transferred to Helen Springs Station on the Barkly Tableland in the Northern Territory. Graeme was to be the head stockman under Tim Doran. Tim was the first Vestey Station manager Graeme worked for at Manbulloo Station near Katherine and in that time, he, his wife Joc and Graeme had become firm friends. Thus, we decided we would have another crack at 'tying the knot' in the beautiful gardens of Helen Springs.

CHAPTER 11

The Bush wedding at Helen Springs and other stuff

Our wedding date was set for the 16 April 1974 on Helen Springs Station, coinciding with the Renner Springs races and rodeo. We picked the last day of the 'meeting' to wed because we figured we'd have sufficient time to pack up the race meeting camp and move back to the station homestead in the morning. That would leave us the afternoon free for celebrant and celebration.

Immediately prior to the Renner Springs Race/Rodeo meeting, both Graeme and I were injured. He was thrown from a racehorse during training and knocked out cold while I was chucked off a milker's poddy calf, straining a calf muscle (no pun intended). Graeme sported a couple of inches of gravel rash down the side of his face and I walked with a pronounced limp. The fact we probably looked as if we had been embroiled in a nasty physical altercation did little to enhance the solemnity of our nuptials!

My friend Carol, wife of the fencing contractor Ron who had sat out the 'wet' with us at Flora Valley, made my bridal gown for me. It was plain white to the floor with long sleeves and polo neck. No veil, no fancy hairdo for me. My long hair had to serve as a veil! No bouquet of flowers either. Just me with the flies.

The Elliot policeman's wife made our wedding cake. She did a sterling job and in a spurt of creativity, or more likely a burst of 'making do', she employed the use of sherry glasses on which to stand the second layer instead of the ornamental pillars found on most conventional wedding cakes. Those were hard to come by on the Barkly Tablelands.

The morning of our wedding was hectic. We packed up the Renner Springs race meeting camp and trundled back to the station, worn out from four days of hard riding, celebration and general partying. After lunch, the station population began to amble towards the showers and 'best' clothes, which hung barely touched in cupboards for months at a time and were now laid out in preparation for our two o'clock wedding. The telephone rang incessantly, many of the calls coming from well-wishers far and wide. As no one was manning the office at the time I answered most of these calls myself. In fact, I was so engaged in this task, I almost

Chapter 11 The Bush wedding at Helen Springs and other stuff

forgot the time. It was only when a young jackaroo pelted up the path, freshly damp from his shower and struggling manfully with an uncooperative tie that I remembered. I was to be married in ten minutes time!

No flower girls or bridesmaids to fuss over and assist this bride. I simply did what I did nearly every day of the week — changed out of my jeans and shirt, in and out of the shower, but this time into a bridal gown. A dab of make-up, a hasty hair brush and I made my way out onto the lawn where the station personnel had assembled.

I don't remember a lot about our wedding, but what recollections remain are colourful! Best man Tim standing beside my husband-to-be, casually tossing my wedding ring from one hand to the other in a best attempt to drop it in the grass and lose it! Fortunately, he didn't succeed. Then there was the dog that chose a critically solemn moment during our exchange of vows to drag its bottom across the lawn right where we could see it. How does one *not* burst out laughing at such a sight but we handled ourselves quite well, I thought.

Last, but best of all was the romantic moment when Graeme and I were asked to face each other, hold hands, look into one another's eyes and make our vows. I was lucky. I got through mine without any interruptions, but when Graeme began his vows, a fly settled on the corner of his mouth. Mesmerised, I watched it slowly make tracks uphill, stopping to investigate his grazed cheek before moseying on towards his eye via his left nostril.

'I, Graeme (phoo) Francis Wicks do take you (phoo) Valerie (phoo) Judith Hames to be my lawfully wedded bride, to have and to hold, in (phooo) sickness and in health, for richer or poorer, now and (phooo) for ever until death do us part.' As if to punctuate his sentence, Graeme took a swipe at the fly with barely restrained frustration. It's a wonder he didn't knock his eye out, but the fly, as flies mostly do, escaped unscathed. The ring Tim didn't drop on the lawn and have to forage for was placed on my finger. The dog with its itchy bum temporarily relieved lay peacefully nearby and we were pronounced man and wife. When I think of our wedding ceremony, I can't help coining a phrase from *Brer Rabbit* by Joel Chandler Harris — it was all a 'monstrous gigglement'.

A barbeque tea was held for our reception and the wedding cake was paraded out with all the pomp and ceremony one might expect on such an occasion. However, the heat had got to it and the sherry glasses were sinking at various depths into the rapidly softening creation. The top layer leaned precariously to one side and the whole construction took on a decidedly boozy appearance. As night fell, we sat around the barbeque enjoying each other's company. I hadn't noticed the stealthy disappearance of a number of jackaroos — they simply melted into the dark, but it was Tim who approached us when we were ready to leave.

'Your ute has been tied up with so much toilet paper and

Chapter 11 The Bush wedding at Helen Springs and other stuff

Graeme and I wed in Helen Springs garden.

old tins,' he told us, 'I doubt you'll be able to move it tonight. Here, take the keys to our car and head off in that.'

'Heading off' didn't mean to a honeymoon on some romantic beach. It was to a deserted house at a deserted road transport base on the ridge that overlooked Helen Springs Station up on the Stuart highway, about 6 km away.

*Honey moon house, No. 1 bore and stock yards,
Helen Springs station.*

I felt rather mean-spirited as Graeme and I snuck into the shadows towards Tim's car. I remember seeing figures running out of the dark towards us as the engine fired, disappointment etched on their faces as we drove away. I didn't feel sorry for them for long. They had their day. It took us so long to make the utility both movable and presentable again I thought it would rust before we got done; the boys had done a very thorough job. And if that weren't enough, they also uncovered our 'secret' location.

The peace and quiet of our first honeymoon night was noisily disrupted an hour or so after we arrived and settled down to sleep. Len, the little Mexican-looking bloke who

Chapter 11 The Bush wedding at Helen Springs and other stuff

drove me from Spring Creek to Nicholson all those months before was now Helen Springs' Overseer and had sniffed out our whereabouts. He arrived with a carton of beer, a bucket of rocks and the jackaroos we thwarted earlier. He and his band of merry men threw the rocks on the roof and then kept us out of bed for the next couple hours while they happily absorbed the carton of beer and told exaggerated yarns of one-upmanship with some lewd 'honeymoon jokes' thrown in for good measure.

Early next morning, we stocked and packed up the stock camp trailer with swags [22] and provisions ready to head out to No. 1 bore. This was our first mustering camp as newlyweds. The fact we had no honeymoon didn't concern us at all. We were both keen to 'go bush' and get started and we had our honeymoon at the end of 1974 when we saved up holidays (and money) to travel to Rhodesia to see my parents. It was the best thing we could have done. Mum and Dad gave us a Flame Lily tour for a wedding present and it was the first time I really got to appreciate the country I had inhabited for seventeen years. How true it is that one seldom gets to enjoy the tourist attractions of the country one lives in.

It was at No. 8 bore that my spiritual journey began in earnest. I had become so immersed in my New Testament that I even burned the dinner I was preparing for the stock camp on one occasion. I had found a treasure trove of

---
22 Bedrolls

wisdom I never knew was available to me even though a drawer full of Bibles existed in our house in Rhodesia, and I had become convinced of the reality of a God who not only created the universe and everything in it but had also paid a terrible price to save us from ourselves. This may not make much sense to some any more than the belief that everything evolved from a single cell coming from nothing and arriving from nowhere without a purpose makes sense to me. However, my life began changing in a most positive way after I made my commitment to a God I could 'feel' but not see, except through what I now believed He had made.

Three men from a church in Sydney with whom I had been corresponding made an epic trip to Helen Springs to seek me out. Being far from the station homestead at No. 8 bore, I feel it was providence that led them to me, with a little assistance from the mud map Len scratched in the dirt with the toe of his boot. These intrepid travellers followed fences and indistinct roads and were forced to spend the night on the open downs at No. 10 bore, about 16 km from No. 8. Just three Sydneysiders camping in the middle of nowhere was almost miraculous!

Graeme was away when they rolled into our camp the next morning and I'm not sure he looked favourably on his wife sitting around the campfire in the company of three strange men with Bibles on their knees. He discreetly disappeared and left me to my questioning. After receiving

Chapter 11 The Bush wedding at Helen Springs and other stuff

answers to every question that had been on my mind for so long directly from the scriptures, it became clear that I needed to be immersed in water for the forgiveness of my many sins. The three men and I traipsed up the banks of the turkey's nest[23] and I was baptised 'into Christ' as the scriptures commanded.

Being winter and out on wide-open downs, very cold winds often prevail. We used to call them 'lazy winds' as they drove straight through a body and never went round. We emerged from the 'baptismal font' and almost froze solid before reaching the fire, which was in an old wood stove we were using. It had gone out so, in my haste to get it started again, I threw a splash of kerosene onto the white-hot ash. Fire exploded from the firebox, instantly relieving me of my eyebrows and eyelashes and leaving the skin on my face feeling scorched and tender. I remember how we joked that it was just as well I was now saved.

After my three new friends had departed on their return journey to Sydney, Graeme began asking questions concerning what I had learned and why I had been baptised. He had grown up in a more religious environment than me with a devout Presbyterian mother and had been christened as a baby before he was old enough to know which way was up. He attended Sunday school quite often and had wondered many times what lay beyond the skies and speculated on the 'why am I here?' question many

---

23 A large raised water storage tank with earth walls

people ask at certain times in their lives. I had also had a bit of water splashed on my head as an infant but otherwise, church attendance was limited strictly to weddings and funerals, until I got to St Pious.

I shared everything I knew and had learned from the scriptures with Graeme. He soaked it up like a dry sponge and I was elated when he asked to be baptised as well. Elated but apprehensive since there was no priest or padre to oversee the procedure. It was going to be up to me to conduct the formality so we waded into the turkey's nest together. When weeds closed over his face and I couldn't see him in the murky water anymore, a jolt of fear rose in my chest but he emerged from his watery grave adorned with algae and slime and we were able to embark on our spiritual and earthly journeys together.

Over time, my use of profanity ceased, as did my overindulgence in alcohol both of which God warns against. Some folks have subsequently questioned how anyone can have a good time at a party without getting sloshed. To me, it was rather nice to be able to wake up in the morning and remember not only the party but be able to entertain other participants with vivid descriptions of their activities while under the influence. Besides, if 'science' is true and alcohol kills brain cells, I couldn't justify killing off any more than I already had.

Giving up on the cigarettes took a lot longer — about five years if I remember correctly but smoking wasn't to be found

Chapter 11 The Bush wedding at Helen Springs and other stuff

anywhere in scriptures that I could see so I was probably finding excuses *not* to quit. Nevertheless, when science began revealing links between smoking and lung cancer, I set to work on giving it away more seriously, occasionally bumming[24] a drag from someone else's cigarette until the habit was conquered. The final nail in its coffin was when I gave away my pure silver lighter that had been gifted to me on my twenty-first birthday. I also became calmer within myself and started to see God's handiwork everywhere I looked. I lost the low self-esteem that had plagued my life and began to believe I was created for a purpose by an almighty God and as the old saying goes 'God don't make junk.'

In spite of being closer to civilisation than the Kimberly properties we had worked on, social events were still relatively few. Because one had to gear up for a full weekend due to distance, we were resourceful in making our own entertainment.

The 'bush Olympics' was a favourite amongst the younger crew but there was no age limit. If one thought one was up to the rigours of it, one had a go and blow the consequences. These 'games' were usually preceded by sufficient grog to numb the effects of any negative outcomes anyway. The sack race and three-legged race, amusing spectacles under sober conditions transformed into helpless hilarity when the importance of sobriety had been thrown out the window. The goanna pull was a test of strength but not necessarily

---

24 Scrounging

an accurate one. On hands and knees, two competitors were linked face to face by a belt around their necks and their goal was to drag each other backwards across a line scratched in the dirt. No rules or weight limits, if Tom Thumb wanted to pit himself against Hercules, all good and no one cared who won.

Helen Springs had a well-maintained tennis court with night lights and we often sallied out to play a set or two in the evening after tea. One particularly unforgettable game, as I recall it, was after we had all helped Willy, one of the stockmen, to celebrate his birthday by consuming a bottle of what I dubbed as 'curly' wine. The bottle had a long, corkscrew sort of neck perhaps sixty centimetres long and made pouring the beverage into glasses quite challenging. It also tested the wits and sobriety of anyone who might want to drink straight from the bottle. After we had drained the last drop, we traipsed out to the court. Wimbledon could never keep up with the standard of play that night. One player asked which ball he had to hit because he said there were three of them coming at him all at once and another doubles match ended in a draw because neither pair could beat their opponents.

Another game was invented off the cuff when we were helping the overseer either pack or renovate. Of course, it was hot work and there was beer all round. Then someone discovered a marble under a mat. I don't remember who kicked off the idea but we all took turns standing over an

Chapter 11 The Bush wedding at Helen Springs and other stuff

empty beer bottle and trying to drop the marble in the bottle from head height. Some of us could occasionally hit the mark but Rhonda from Tennant Creek station managed to do it three times in a row. Perhaps she hadn't been cooling off with the long cold lagers as much as the rest of us.

I hadn't been in Australia very long when I was introduced to 'camp drafting'. A group of us from Nicholson travelled to the Renner Springs races and rodeo located a short distance from Helen Springs where Tim and Joc were managing at the time.

On the day of the rodeo Tim asked if I'd like to participate in the camp draft. I'd never seen or heard of such a thing before so he explained how it all worked and said he had a really old, quiet horse I could cut my camp drafting teeth on. When he introduced me to Sambo, I wondered how the horse could possibly run fast enough to push cattle at a gallop around a set course. Black and hairy, he was quite small and looked 'old'. That's all I remember of his appearance but his agility will live with me forever.

Last minute instructions while Tim tightened the girth — 'Just hang on tight. Sambo knows what to do.' In hindsight, I was sorry Sambo hadn't let me in on the secret too. Into the drafting pen we went and I looked diligently for an animal I thought might be amenable to being bullied around an obstacle course when it would rather lie down in a shady spot somewhere. I'm not sure I got as far as picking one. Faster than a cat on a rat, that 'really old, quiet horse' had a steer drafted out and into the arena all on his own while I sat in the middle of the drafting pen red in the face and thinking 'So that's how camp drafting works.' A somewhat inauspicious start to my camp drafting experience, there was only room for improvement and while I don't recall ever winning a place in one, I managed to stay in the saddle and began to look as if I knew a *little* of what I was doing. On the other hand, the horses I rode in camp drafting knew everything there was to know about it and forever and a day I was only the passenger, never the pilot.

It was at Helen Springs that I experienced my first ever frightening night time incident and hopefully my last.

Graeme was away for a few days out on the bore run so I was home alone. It was just days before the Renner Springs races-rodeo and overseer Len and I were rising well before daylight to work the horses already ensconced at the racecourse (the same little 'Mexican' Len previously mentioned).

It was a hot night and I had been asleep for several hours with my ceiling fan working full lick when our dog Mac started barking. This was unusual for him and I groggily cocked an ear to listen. A dog from the Aboriginal camp responded. Then Mac barked again. Thinking he was just talking to the camp dog, I walked outside and yelled at him to 'shut up.' Back in bed, I was lying on my side with my back towards the door when I felt my top sheet move. This sometimes occurred when the breeze from the fan captured

Chapter 11 The Bush wedding at Helen Springs and other stuff

a corner and fluttered it gently so I turned over to pin the sheet down. There was a hand under my back! My eyes flew open in time to see a short silhouette bounding through the door into the night. The stature was similar to that of Len and I remember saying 'Oh Len!' with exasperation as he'd scared me half to death. This was exactly the sort of prank he would pull though, even though he was now married so I figured it was his way of waking me to go and work the race horses. Must be four o'clock. Dressing quickly, I stepped outside and looked up at Len's house expecting to see lights on and signs of life. There was nothing. The entire station was wrapped in a blanket of darkness and silence. Confused, I checked the clock on the wall. Two in the morning?

'Must have stopped,' I thought but the clock beside my bed also indicated it was only 2 am. I realised then there was some form of pervert lurking somewhere. If he had been watching me close by, Mac wasn't going to say anything since I'd scolded him for barking not half an hour before. Poor dog was trying to warn me but we were so used to being secure from this sort of activity, I took no notice of him.

Any chance of going back to sleep for the next two hours was gone and I lay awake listening to every night sound. Imaginary dangers kept me occupied until I rose again at 4 am. This time Len's house was ablaze with light and he was waiting for me to arrive. I told him what had happened and he must have passed the news on to Tim straight away because we arrived home for breakfast to the sound of banging in my house. Tim was putting a bolt on my door where no bolt had ever been before.

The mystery visitor tried his hand again (no pun intended) another night, this time on Len's wife Raelene who was also alone except for their dog Benson. Benson was accustomed to sleeping right at their front door and the visitor picked a stick, presumably for protection from possible attack. He needn't have worried. Benson wouldn't assault a fly and snored on as the intruder stepped over his sleeping form. Making his way to Raelene's room, it was unfortunate for the prowler that Raelene was not expecting a wake-up call from a prankster. She shot out of bed and chased him back over the dog and into the safety of a pitch-black night before Benson had time to realise anything had happened at all.

CHAPTER 12

More Helen Springs experiences

From this point onwards, recollections of our time at Helen Springs are surely not in consecutive order. In fact, I wouldn't lay bets on any of my memories being in consecutive order.

Our first stock camp as Mr and Mrs Wicks comprised of three young lads who knew nothing about station life, horses or anything else that would have rendered them remotely useful in the scheme of things. It was therefore up to Graeme to teach them and he started a 'riding school' at five o'clock in the afternoon when we finished work for the day. Quiet horses were brought into the yards, and 'The Colonel', as Graeme was nicknamed, taught the boys how to catch and saddle their mounts. This involved not just catching, saddling and riding but also how to keep their tack tidy. Like most teenage boys I ever knew, they had a tendency to leave their gear strewn around if Graeme didn't keep a stern eye on them.

They seemed to be doing quite well one particular evening, one boy already mounted and confidently riding around the yard for several minutes. Graeme finished instructing another lad, then called to the mounted jackaroo.

'Hey, Stretch! Get off your horse and show me how you mount up.'

We will never know what caused Stretch's world to fall apart at that precise moment but when he tried to remount, he placed his right foot into the stirrup iron. It's always easy to realise you've done this. You either have to throw the left leg over the horse's neck and finish up facing its rear end, or you tie yourself in knots trying to get the left leg to swap places with the right one. Whatever resolution you reach, you seldom repeat this mistake a second time but Stretch did. Twice more he put his right foot in the stirrup and the deepening frown of confusion and frustration was enough to make the rest of us rock with ill-disguised laughter! The poor boy finally worked himself out and from then on riding school proceeded without any hitches.

As with Stretch, the two other boys were also nicknamed. 'Gearbox' was a fourteen-year-old lad who made revving noises and 'changed gears' whenever he moved. 'Spider' was named for his legs, not much thicker than a Daddy long-legs spider. 'Stretch' is self-explanatory.

Chapter 12 More Helen Springs experiences

It was apparent that common sense was not something these young lads had a lot of at this early stage of their lives and fencing served only to confuse them further. One old fence had to be pulled out up to a certain point and new fence constructed from then on. To make the job quicker, the boys divided into two teams. One of them and another stockman began building the new fence, while the other two dismantled the old one. Both Tim and Graeme strongly emphasised the need to stop pulling down when they reached the new fence but the message took a detour somewhere. They dismantled the old fence and then cantered happily ahead pulling up the new fence with boyish enthusiasm!

On another occasion, one of the boys dug a posthole at the wrong end of the dropped post, putting it out of line by about two metres. Common sense would have enabled him to see the problem he was making for himself but it didn't so another hole had to be dug with shovel and crowbar in the hard-baked soil.

In 1975, the cessation of certain bodily functions gave rise to the suspicion that I might be pregnant. I had no intention of having a child at that time. In fact, I wasn't sure I wanted any children at all but I married a man who came from a family of seven and wanted at least six children.[25] I finally bundled myself off to Tennant Creek to see the doctor, only to have my suspicions confirmed

---

25 We compromised and had three!

— that I was with child, or 'in calf' as stockmen so delicately put it. In a state of shock, I had just begun the drive home when I noticed the flashing lights of a police car behind me. Vivian, another station employee who came with me for company alerted me to the fact that I didn't have my seat belt on. What I felt at that very moment could be likened to a bunch of Girl Guides practicing knots with my intestines!

A chubby officer sauntered to my door and casually mentioned that he'd noticed my lack of seat belt and did I have any reason for not wearing one? I couldn't think of one on the spur of the moment so he pulled out his pad and began taking down my particulars. Vivian and I sat baking inside the car while the poor officer sweated outside. It was during the officer's trawl for information that Vivian leaned over and quietly told me she'd heard somewhere that pregnant women didn't have to wear seatbelts.

'Ask him,' she encouraged. 'You never know.'

'Excuse me, officer,' I began. 'Is it right that pregnant women don't have to wear seat belts?' There was a 'pregnant pause'. Then the policeman raised his eyes from his pad and stared at me. 'Because,' I continued bravely, 'I'm pregnant.' The poor man carefully put his pen in his pocket. His movements were slow and deliberate as he tucked his clipboard under his arm and removed his hat. Wearily, he wiped the sweat from his face and said 'Lady, you have a good reason for not wearing a seat belt!'

Chapter 12 More Helen Springs experiences

On my return to Helen Springs, I mentioned the incident to Col, the station bookkeeper, also a Justice of the Peace. He laughed, loudly.

'That only applies to women who are four months and over,' he said. I was glad the officer hadn't asked me to 'show my credentials', which were next to none at the time and I felt fortunate that I only had to present my driver's licence at the police station the next time I went to town.

In what must have been a moment of madness that periodically assails pregnant women, I took on the job of horse tailer[26] for the stock camp while Vivian took charge of the camp's cooking. I'm not sure why I put my hand up for this job although I was never a great fan of kitchen duties and far preferred to be on a horse. Ignorance had a lot to do with it. To start with, I didn't know that pregnancy causes considerable pressure on the bladder and the urge to pass water often was something I had to learn to deal with in my capacity as horse tailer. While I never had a hint of morning sickness, I used to feel quite nauseous when I rode one of the tailer's horses at a canter. He had a wonderfully gentle rocking motion and while I never unloaded my dinner, I did sometimes feel I might.

One incident I especially remember is the desperate 'call of nature' in the middle of a flat, treeless plain. The stockmen were ahead of me with a mob of quiet cattle they were using

---

26 One responsible for the horses, catching the stockmen's mounts and following the musterers with fresh horses.

as coaches for cattle we were to muster and I followed behind with fresh horses for dinner camp. The urge to urinate fast outgrew my sense of modesty and I ungracefully dismounted. I had held off as long as I could to put as much distance between the men and me as my bursting bladder would allow. I also had the fresh horses in front of me, so I figured I would be obscured from view. Uncomfortably squatted and feeling a tremendous sense of relief, a quail suddenly fluttered out of the grass directly under my horse's nose. Panic-stricken, she lunged backwards hauling me to my feet. Desperate not to let her go and attract any attention to myself, I stumbled after her with my jeans around my ankles (as if that wouldn't attract attention). Such a hideous apparition compelled the mare to back away even faster and it was all I could do to stay on my feet.

On the cusp of letting the horse go, she stopped suddenly and we both gawked at one another, as still as statues. Her eyes as wide as saucers, her nostrils flared and quivering, she blew trumpeting snorts at me from somewhere above my head as I stood gasping for breath, my bum exposed to the Northern Territory sunshine. Happily, the stockmen had disappeared over a ridge and I could only hope they hadn't looked back at the critical moment to see how I was progressing. If they witnessed any of the riotous spectacle, they must have figured discretion was the better part of valour and declined to mention it.

One beautiful sunny day, the water outlet from the

Chapter 12 More Helen Springs experiences

turkey's nest was blocked and the only way to unblock it was to dive to the bottom and pull the weeds out of the pipe. As I had the ability to stay under water for quite extended periods of time, Tim asked me if I would do the job? Unable to find the outlet by feeling with the feet, I called on Graeme to come and see if he could locate it. Stripping down to his underwear, he joined me in the centre of the turkey's nest.

It was deep and masses of weed floated around our legs as we inched around in search of the blocked pipe. Graeme finally found it and I went to work. Taking a deep breath, I dived. Weeds closed over me and for the first time ever I felt claustrophobic and anxious. I also had been regaled with tales of people who had similarly dived to unblock pipes, had been held fast by the sudden suction as the water let go and were unable to surface for air. The fear of this happening to me used up copious amounts of oxygen in a very short time and I was unable to succeed. Graeme finally unblocked it.

'I'll race you to the bank,' he called when he'd finished. I agreed although I knew he'd beat me. He always did. He didn't have much style as a swimmer, and I probably looked a lot more elegant, but he was definitely faster and always reminded me of Banjo Patterson's poem *The Geebung Polo Club* — He 'had very little style but a mighty lot of dash!' Or perhaps in this case, 'splash'.

I struck out for the bank at my top speed, occasionally glancing back to see where the opposition lay. To my surprise, he remained behind me all the way! When he finally hauled himself on to the bank he was laughing and spluttering as if he'd swallowed a lot of water. Then I saw why. It hadn't been a fair contest. His jocks[27] had slipped off and wound around his ankles, effectively cramping his usually flamboyant and effective freestyle. I should have known something was up. He would never have let me win out of gallantry!

Our days at Helen Springs were filled with many incidents, funny, sad and bad. I still remember so clearly a terrible sound like a gunshot when one of the faithful old mustering horses put his foot in a hole at full gallop after a mob of fleeing bullocks. It was a terrible fall and while overseer Len escaped unhurt, the horse's neck was snapped. It was a sadly solemn occasion as we all stood around the stricken animal, unable to help him. He lay there breathing gently for a few seconds before a deep sigh heralded the end of his life. He was one of the good horses, honest as the day was long and how often I heard the sentiment expressed 'Why couldn't it have happened to that myall[28] chestnut/brown/bay ...?'

Some interesting people came to Helen Springs during our time there, most memorable of whom were 'Gorgeous George', Blue and the 'Blond Bomber'.

George was different to the average stockman we were used to. He was clean-cut with impeccable manners and I

---
27 Underpants
28 Mongrel, stupid, useless

Chapter 12 More Helen Springs experiences

was always startled when he pulled my campstool out for me to sit on, or opened doors for me if there were any to open in the camp. This was a code of conduct I had seen my brothers taught, but had mostly forgotten its existence. Unfortunately, my memory of George has nothing to do with his ability as a stockman or bronc rider. After spending some months in the stock camp, George quite literally disappeared.

He was involved in a car roll-over when we were travelling across the Murrinji stock route to the Negri Picnic Races about 1,000 km away and sustained a nasty bump on his head. The car was unhurt. Approximately a week after the occurrence, we were to take horses to compete at the Daly Waters rodeo and George had his horse and gear packed and ready to go with us. He appeared every bit as keen as the rest of us and if he were hatching a plot, none of us were any the wiser.

The night before leaving for Daly Waters rodeo, we gathered at Tim and Joc's house for drinks. George said he'd be up after he'd fuelled his vehicle and stowed his gear on the back. He never turned up. Nor did he come to the table for tea and the following morning when we were ready to leave, his pony stood alone in the yard and George's bed hadn't been slept in. He didn't collect his pay either, which was perhaps the most unusual of all the incidents leading up to his disappearance.

To this day, we don't know where George went. I still find myself wondering if the bump on his head wasn't more serious than any of us suspected, perhaps causing some sort of amnesia but we're unlikely to know. I often wish he would walk through the door one day and tell us what really happened that night so long ago.

Blue was also a clean-cut young feller with red hair and one glass eye. I never have understood 'Blue' being a common nickname for red-haired people and he was my first encounter with one. Nor had I met anyone with a glass eye before. Blue's tended to point in a slightly different direction to its mate and that rattled me a bit until I grew accustomed to it. It must have been awful for him working in the dust and I know he had to remove the eye frequently to wash both the eye and the socket, though he was always discreet about it.

We were camped at the No. 8 stock camp and Blue had been sent to muster the horses for shoeing. He hadn't been around when the rest of the men found a very large King Brown snake drowned in the cattle dip. They hauled the putrefying creature out and dragged it over to the horse yard, carefully setting it up with its large venomous-head laid amongst the shoeing equipment.

Blue returned with the horses and a little later on began to have trouble shoeing one of his steeds. He being inexperienced, the horse sensed a moment for a bit of fun and proceeded to take the mickey[29] out of him. It fidgeted one minute then leaned as much of its weight on him as

---

29 Tease, test, try the patience.

Chapter 12 More Helen Springs experiences

it could without actually falling over until Blue conceded defeat and let Graeme step in to help.

After a moment of hoof rasping, Graeme asked Blue to fetch a shoe. The unsuspecting lad trotted across to the shoeing gear and picked up a shoe that lay no further than 15 cm from the head of the equally unsuspecting serpent. Giving the shoe to Graeme, Blue glanced at me and another stockman, Willy, alerted no doubt by loud snickers from the top rail of the yard.

'What's up?' he queried. 'Have I got a hole in my strides[30] or something?' We weren't game to answer him for fear of giving the secret away before we'd had a bit more fun with him. Blue gingerly ran his hand over his backside, feeling for what he was now convinced must have been a large hole.

'Okay Blue, can you bring me some nails and the hammer, please,' Graeme called out. Again, Blue picked up the required material while the vacant dead eyes of the snake glared vindictively at him, reproachful that it hadn't been noticed. This was too much for Willy and I, who clung precariously to the top rail, tears of laughter making pale tracks through the dust on our faces. Poor Blue was a picture of consternation until Graeme asked him to go and pick up the snake.

'Snake?' he yelled. 'What snake?' When his one eye finally met the reptile's two dead ones across the yard, Blue was galvanised into a spasmodic 'will I-won't I' action! Snatching up a thirty-centimetre shoeing hammer, he

---

30 Jeans, long pants

proceeded to beat the decomposing serpent until he realised that he'd been 'had'. I can't remember what he said then, or if he said anything at all. I just have the feeling it would have included a few full-bodied expletives if he did.

Manager Tim began hiring women to work in the stock camps long before this trend became fashionable and so entered the 'Blond Bomber'. For one who evokes funny memories, I can't remember her real name and that may be just as well. The Bomber was probably a sight for a bunch of stockmen's sore eyes, although no woman would have had to try very hard. As I remember, she was quite tall and voluptuous but perhaps I should stop there. I remember thinking at the time she had the appearance of seeing and knowing a lot about the birds and the bees, perhaps even profiting from that knowledge at some stage in her life. Willing to give her the benefit of the doubt, it wasn't long before she made moves to wriggle her way into every stockman's swag. She was quite transparent about it all, as if she thought this was normal every night practice. Even my newly married husband wasn't out of bounds. Whether she succeeded with the other blokes is unknown to me, but there's one feller I know she didn't get!

The mind can do some amazing things and we were working on Helen Springs when I came face to face with what had been a moment of 'mental aberration' and which only mysteriously came halfway to resolving itself well over a year later.

Chapter 12 More Helen Springs experiences

Being a jeweller in Buenos Aires, my maternal grandfather had created a beautiful sapphire ring for my mother's twenty-first birthday. Made from white gold with a single sapphire and two small diamonds either side, this ring was handed down to me on my twenty-first birthday. I had taken to wearing this instead of my engagement ring as it had flat-set stones. The stones on the engagement ring stood too high for practicality and had a tendency to get caught up on things.

I was setting off on a long trip to pick up a horse from another Vestey station. I don't remember which horse nor which station but I vaguely recall Joc, Tim's wife accompanying me. For some reason, I took my sapphire ring off and tucked it into a pocket in my 'man-style' wallet which folded in half but left the pocket openings exposed. I'd dare to say many a coin has been lost from a man's wallet, though this may not be true since men's wallets are usually carried in a back pocket tight up against the gluteus maximus.

We drove to the west across the rough Murrinji Road and the trip was uneventful until after we arrived back home and I remembered, and looked for, my heirloom ring in the pocket of my wallet. It wasn't there. I searched through every pocket twice and the certainty that it was missing sent a chill through me. How was I going to tell my mother?

I thought of many possibilities for the loss of this precious piece of jewellery but one made more sense to me than others. My wallet had lain on the seat between Joc and me, and if I had been careless and let the open pockets face down-hill toward the back of the seat, it was possible the ring had slipped out and jiggled through the crack onto the floor as we bumped over the Murrinji Road. Excitedly, I moved the seats forward and peered underneath with the use of a torch to light up the dark areas. There was no sign of a ring to gladden my heart but there were quite large drainage holes on the floor beneath the seats that led to the outside world. My heart sunk like a stone. Feeling certain my ring now lay somewhere on the hundreds of kilometres of rough dirt road we had crossed I gave up the search. When Graeme and I travelled to Rhodesia at the end of the year to visit my family I couldn't pluck up enough courage to tell my mum I had lost the heirloom ring.

I don't remember how long it was before we were preparing to leave Helen Springs but it was well over twelve months since the ring had disappeared. I had finished mourning its loss and although I never completely forgot about it, out of sight was largely out of mind.

I was working on cleaning out the top drawer of our chest of drawers and because my drawers tend to collect all manner of bits and largely useless pieces, I had a habit of putting anything I didn't need immediately into a plastic bag and stuffing it into the back of the drawer. When it came to tidying the drawer, I would rummage through the bag and perform another cull on the bric-a-brac hoarded inside.

Pulling the plastic bag into the light of day, I noticed a

Chapter 12 More Helen Springs experiences

tightly balled-up piece of tissue paper wedged into a corner of the bag.

'Good night! Surely not a snotty tissue?' I thought. I can imagine myself doing something like that in my advancing years but not when I was in my thirties surely? I pulled the wad of paper out and opened it up carefully, half expecting to see nothing of any consequence. My heirloom ring lay nestled in the creased paper and my heart almost stopped! How could that possibly have got there?

There never was an answer to that question. I would have sworn on every Bible in the land that I had put that ring in my wallet and what really happened has never been revealed, as brains sometimes eventually do. All I am left with is an utterly inexplicable anomaly.

The ring has a new home now, handed down to my daughter Megan. If she manages not to lose it, it will eventually be passed on to my granddaughter, Joanne.

Chapter 13

Vestey's gypsies

A period of time followed when cattle prices plummeted and things were not going well for those involved in the cattle industry. Because Graeme was a good head stockman, Vestey wanted to keep him on the books, even if it meant shifting him to any position at any time and shift us, they did!

I was four months pregnant with our first child when this began and I was grateful that all the goods and chattels we possessed fitted snugly in the back of Graeme's Dodge utility. I don't remember how many times we had to pack up and move to another Vestey station in a period of some eighteen months but the figure twelve pops into mind.

One of these interim positions for Graeme was as bore mechanic on Nutwood Downs Station near Daly Waters in the Northern Territory. Another was catering for a horse sale held at Wave Hill Station over a period of four days. Graeme was also asked to stand in as manager at Limbunya Station for a short time, be overseer at Spring Creek Station for several weeks, then to run the camp at Manbulloo near Katherine where his Territory experiences first commenced until the new head stockman arrived. Then it was back to Helen Springs to be head stockman until a new one was located. Bearing in mind there were many hundreds of kilometres between each of these jobs, it's hard to see why we didn't become mentally unhinged. I suppose we were young, resilient and just too thankful to be employed. The tension we were obviously feeling did raise its ugly head during our trip from Helen Springs to the Wave Hill horse sale, though.

We had a dog called Mac, a black and white Kelpie cross that had been with me since he was a puppy and he accompanied us on our travels hither and thither, comfortably bedded down in the back of the ute. These were the days before dogs were expected to be tied on the back or in cages and Mac was free of restraint. We had not long turned off the highway onto the Murrinji dirt road when I discovered that Mac was missing. I asked Graeme to turn back and at least go as far as the Dunmara Roadhouse so I could post a LOST notice on its windows if we didn't find Mac in the meantime. Needless to say, Graeme wasn't impressed and a difficult silence accompanied us back to the highway. There was still no sign of the dog and Graeme announced that he wasn't prepared to go the last few kilometres to the roadhouse. I could scarcely believe my ears! The Dunmara Roadhouse was no more than 4 or perhaps 5 km down the road, just around a corner. I pled with him. I even argued that there were no windows right here for me to post any notices on but it made no difference. Graeme had resolved to go no further so I got mad!

'OK,' I hissed. Flinging open the car door, I stepped out into the hot Territory sunshine. 'I'll walk there. I suppose I'll see you later.' Slamming the door to make an impression like a petulant child, I stomped off down the bitumen. I heard the old ute's motor bellow and a quick glance out of the corner of my eye revealed the car doing a roaring wheelie to head back the way we had come, towards Wave Hill Station.

'Now you've done it,' I thought. 'He's actually going to leave you.' However, concern for my dog and the fact I really needed a toilet drove me on towards the roadhouse without another backward glance.

Several cars stopped to ask if I needed a lift. The sight of a now obviously pregnant white woman waddling down the highway in the middle of the Northern Territory must have caused some consternation, and even cars coming from the direction I was heading stopped to ask if they could help. Being well aware of stranger danger, I refused all offers of a lift but asked them all to please keep an eye open for my dog.

I had not long walked around the bend in the road when I heard another vehicle pull up behind me. Turning

Chapter 13 Vestey's gypsies

round, I was amazed and secretly *very* relieved to see Graeme stepping out from the back seat with what looked suspiciously like a piece off the ute's motor in his hand.

'Take this and see if you can get another one,' he grunted, steadfastly refusing to catch my eye. 'I'll walk back, you go with them,' and he propelled me into the back seat of the waiting vehicle.

It was a relief to reach the roadhouse in more ways than one. I posted my notice on the window, attended a high-pressure 'call of nature' and showed the problem bit of motor vehicle to the resident mechanic. He gave me a lift back to my stricken husband and vehicle and in no time at all he had us back on the Murrinji Road headed to Wave Hill Station.

It was a long and silent trip entirely devoid of conversation. I was annoyed with myself for acting the way I did, but my anxiety for Mac over-rode that emotion to a great extent. If I was able to know the dog had perished in the fall from the ute, I could have accepted it. I just couldn't bear the thought that he might be lying on the side of the road badly injured and unable to move to find food or water. The intense heat would have killed him slowly and painfully *if* he escaped being attacked and killed by dingoes first. From that perspective, I felt I had done the right thing even though Graeme was now furious with me. During that long haul across the dusty Murrinji, I sadly reconciled myself to the possibility that not only might I be facing divorce but it was unlikely I would ever see Mac again.

My surprise and joy when a phone call from the Dunmara Roadhouse the next day informing me Mac had been found can't be described in words! I rushed off to locate Graeme and told him I *had* to go all the way back and collect my pet. The news went over like a lead balloon of course, as I knew it probably would but I didn't stop to think he might be worried about me travelling almost 500 km by myself in my pregnant state. I was suffering from tunnel vision with only one thought in mind — to retrieve my dog. I cringe a little now when I remember all this! No wonder some husbands feel they rate lower than the family pet!

I eventually made the trip to the roadhouse on my own. Mac was lying in the men's toilet where it was cool. I was so relieved because the possibility that the dog might not be Mac at all would have seen me heading south to Alice Springs, or Adelaide! One back leg was broken and he looked a sorry sight indeed but he wagged his tail at the sound of my voice and dragged himself to his feet to greet me. I was ecstatic! On returning to Wave Hill, one of the several vets on hand at the horse sale examined the leg and then plastered it. During the period the plaster was supposed to stay on Graeme and I replaced it several times as the dog would make a beeline for any available waterhole and plonk himself down with goofy gusto. The leg healed well and apart from a slightly more bent appearance it wasn't easy to notice there had been a break there at all.

Chapter 13   Vestey's gypsies

These were interesting times, during which my first baby, a 9 lb 9 oz boy we named Sean and nicknamed Little Lobby due to his ruddy appearance, arrived. We were on Spring Creek Station at the time and the wet season was in full swing. The rivers both sides of us were uncrossable and I later heard that almost every station was on 'red alert' for this pregnant female who was due to give birth. Water Resources in Kununurra had allegedly promised the use of their helicopter if an emergency arose since we were blocked off from the nearest airstrip and, quite unbeknownst to me, I was the cause of considerable anxiety. I, on the other hand, sailed breezily through my pregnancy without much thought! It wasn't like that for the first four months though, and not because of morning sickness either. That was something I was fortunate never to experience for longer than a week.

Because this baby came as a result of some misjudgement, or mismanagement ... or both, I closed my mind to the fact that I could possibly even be pregnant. Even after the Tennant Creek doctor announced that I was to be a mother, I didn't believe it and embarrassed as I am to admit it now, I convinced myself that I probably only had a tumour growing and that all would be revealed in due course. I was right. The tumour began to kick and engage in a line of other manoeuvres even I knew a tumour couldn't do and I was forced to accept that motherhood was well on the way. I had so few maternal instincts at this time, I plucked at the sleeve of one of the travelling nurses one day and poured out my feelings to her.

'I just don't feel anything for this child,' I moaned. 'I should be happy, but I'm devastated! And I keep hearing all these horrible stories about how the baby is given to the mother all yukky right after it's born so the mother can count all its fingers and toes. I don't care about its fingers and toes! I just want it to go away.'

The nurse laughed at me, but she must have detected a hint of desperation in my face and voice because she pulled herself together and patted my arm.

'Val, don't worry about it now,' she soothed. 'You're going to have to have this baby because you can't send it back. If you still feel this way *after* the birth, give me a call. We can talk about it then.'

It was several weeks before I was due to give birth that the rivers finally lowered sufficiently for a vehicle from neighbouring Waterloo Station to cross over to us. Our Spring Creek vehicle had broken down before we arrived and we'd been left without any transport other than our own Holden Station wagon, completely unsuitable for rough terrain. It was decided we would go to Kununurra to replenish badly needed supplies and I would remain there until my confinement.

The Anglican Church in Kununurra had a 'granny flat' built under the minister's residence that was used by outback people like me. Keith was the minister at the

Chapter 13 Vestey's gypsies

time and he and his wife took me in and made me feel very much at home. I hated watching Graeme depart and not knowing how long I would have to remain in Kununurra also disturbed me. Like old piker[31] bullocks that are finally captured and contained, I found myself gazing longingly over the back fence towards where I thought Spring Creek was and pining. Knowing my terrible sense of direction, I was probably pining towards Mecca!

I spent six weeks in the Anglican church's granny flat during which time I made a few new friends. I really don't remember how I passed the time but I recall people dishing out all sorts of good advice about babies, having them, raising them, feeding them and anything that wasn't mentioned probably wasn't worth knowing. One classic piece of advice came from a woman who had been visiting Keith's wife. She had almost got into her car to leave when she suddenly stopped. Then she came back and found me.

'I almost forgot to tell you,' she said. 'When you're in labour always remember to grunt though your bottom'. I was getting used to 'pregnant pauses' by this time and here was another one!

'How exactly do you mean?' I finally asked.

'Well,' she explained, 'when women give birth, they quite often yell and a lot of air escapes through their mouths. This takes pressure away from the area where you really want it

---

[31] Old and cunning beast that had escaped many musters to the meatworks.

to be. Try it,' she encouraged. 'Strain as though you want to push something out but yell at the same time, then do it again but keep your mouth shut and see the difference.'

I couldn't bring myself to experiment in the good lady's presence but promised her I'd take her advice very seriously. After she was gone and when I knew no one else was in the house I tentatively tried and found that she was right. It's remarkable how much extra pressure one can exert on one's nether regions by keeping one's mouth shut. Is there a moral in that somewhere, I wondered?

I developed a tummy ache in the afternoon of 30 March 1976 but didn't take much notice and really didn't think about 'labour'. Being a new chum at all this, I didn't really think it was labour. By nightfall, it wasn't any better so I took a couple of pain killers and retired to bed, thinking that all would be well. All might have been 'well' to one who knows about these things but not from my perspective. The pain became increasingly severe so at 1.30 am I sheepishly climbed the stairs and woke Keith. He drove me to the hospital and I was placed in the delivery ward.

I don't remember a lot of detail here. I don't remember having a 'show', which all the experts kept telling me to expect and my water didn't break to signal that labour was on the way. What I do remember was contractions, agonising and without any breaks in between at all and because of the lack of pauses, I didn't know whether I was having a contraction or not — it was just one long pain!

Chapter 13 Vestey's gypsies

Graeme was notified that I was in labour and he arrived at the hospital sometime in the morning. He did a great job of mopping my face and when we finally moved into the 'pushing' stage, he would tell me when I was having a contraction by watching my stomach bunching like a mole emerging from the ground. Otherwise, I wouldn't have known and wouldn't have pushed either, since I had no urge to push at all. This was *not* a textbook labour by my standards, based on the experts' opinions.

After pushing fruitlessly for what seemed like hours, the doctor paid a visit and discovered the baby's path

The only photo we have of Sean as a baby at Nutwood Station.

was blocked because my waters hadn't broken. Once he attended to that, it didn't take long for Sean to make his entrance into the world, bawling lustily.

'This one is going to be the Prime Minister of Australia,' said Dr Drake, who was responsible for Sean's safe arrival.

You'll remember my fears concerning my lack of motherly instinct? Well, a change I wasn't expecting at all came over me at the moment our baby son emerged. All I wanted to do was to see that child and make sure he was 'complete'! If anyone had tried to remove the baby to bath him so he wouldn't be 'yukky' as I'd so feared, I believe I would have been off the bed and hotfooting it after him like a worried old cow. Thus, I came face to face with the miracle of birth; the changes it wreaks in one's life and the two jets of milk that would squirt three feet at the sound of a baby's cry when I was in the shower! From one who hadn't been keen to have children, I became a lactating, ga-ga mother who would trample underfoot anyone or anything that represented a threat to her offspring.

CHAPTER 14

Mistake Creek Station

In the years that followed, our second son was born and caused much excitement at the Kununurra hospital. Daniel James weighed in at 12 lb 4 oz and was the largest baby ever born there up to that time. He played 'hard to get' from start to finish and I still remember the Wicks' doctor in Kingaroy advising us that 'You'll just have to try harder' when we approached him to find out why things weren't going the way we'd been hoping.

We were employed as managers on Mistake Creek Station by this time and 'trying harder' produced the results we were wishing for. My belly expanded well beyond what was considered normal and there was speculation that I might be carrying twins. Or that I'd got my dates mixed up and would give birth a month or two earlier than calculated. Before the use of ultrasound, X-rays were employed on pregnant women to determine what was going on in the womb but were avoided as much as possible as there was concern that they might harm the developing child. My first X-ray showed only one *large* infant with his head up and bottom down. I was assured he would find his way into the right position by himself but he apparently didn't know that and had no intention of being so amenable so the doctor had to turn him round manually. He was already an uncomfortably tight fit and the procedure was unpleasant though not painful as I recall.

Once Daniel was head down it was reckoned that he wouldn't be able to turn himself round again. The experts were wrong and I had to endure having him manipulated into the head down position a second time. It was much more difficult and a great deal tighter than it had been before and I hoped fervently that he would do what he was told and give no further trouble.

As if to make it up to me, Daniel's birth was as close to 'textbook' as a birth could possibly be in spite of his size. I had the 'show', although it came a week before the birth. Then my waters broke as I stepped out of my car at the hospital. Labour pains came and went in waves, allowing moments of respite in between like the textbooks said, and the whole business from start to finish was done and dusted in six hours. My lovely doctor Fred was so impressed, he brought me a bunch of Jasmine picked from his own garden.

News of our arrival back at Mistake Creek didn't

Chapter 14 Mistake Creek Station

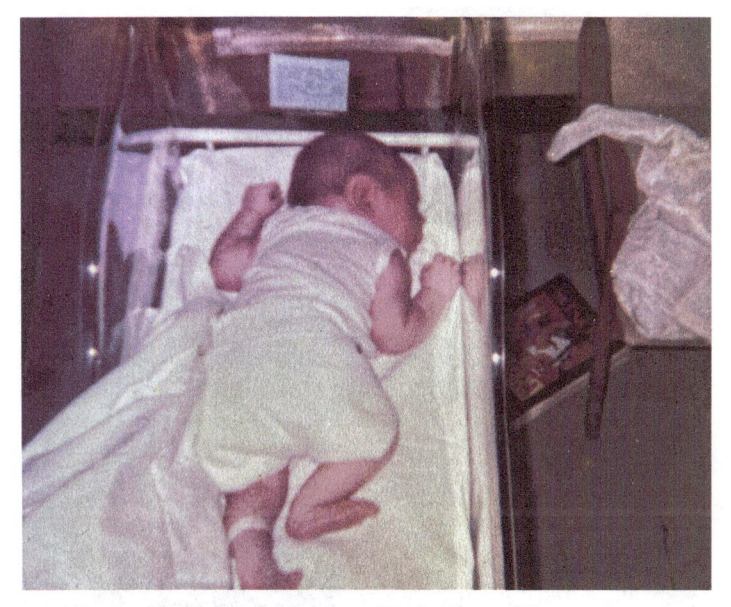

Baby Daniel 2 hours after birth, 12 lbs 4 oz.

take long to spread and I soon had a group of Aboriginal women, most of whom worked for me as kitchen and garden staff, clucking around the enormous baby that looked to be already two months old. The girls were so good with children and I knew I never had to worry about my little brood while ever they were in the vicinity.

Daniel was a bit over two months old when we headed south for our annual holiday and this time we flew. Keeping young Sean occupied and/or in sight was a stimulating exercise as we waited in Darwin airport for our flight south. He kept sliding down the row of seats we were on and, at the moment we chose to be distracted, he disappeared. Fortunately, we could hear him chatting away to someone

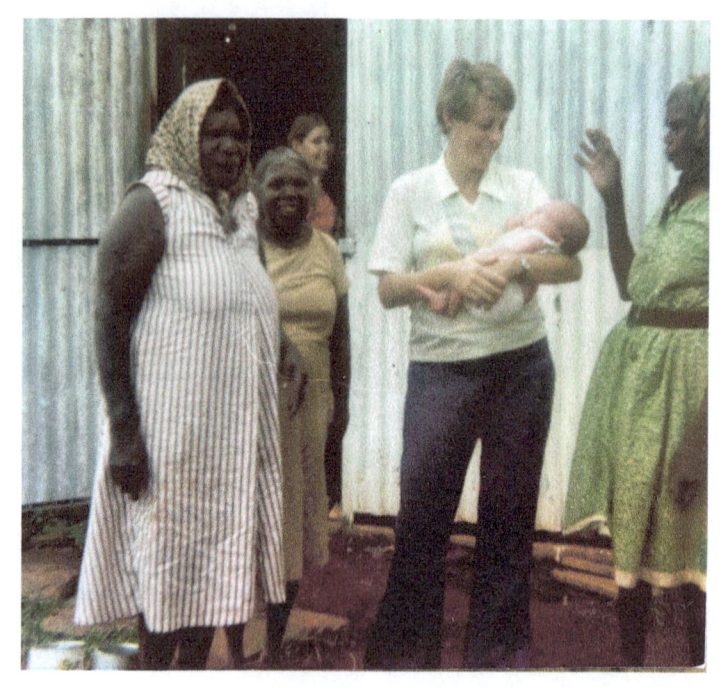

*The Mistake Creek girls come to welcome Daniel.
L_R Dolly, Ikey, Joanne, me, Daniel and Molly.*

who was sitting on the row of seats behind us. This lady was eating something that Sean thought looked delectable. Prattling away about nothing, he leaned in closer and closer towards the woman's food like a dog on the scrounge. We apologised profusely as we retrieved him and assured the lady that we really did feed the boy. Thankfully she was amused, both by Sean's antics and his gift of the gab which he carries with him to this day.

More embarrassing for me than that incident was Daniel. He was an extremely noisy sucker and it wouldn't have

Chapter 14 Mistake Creek Station

mattered if they had put us in the cargo compartment, Daniel would still have been audible from cockpit to the tail of the plane and beyond, greedily appreciating his 'booby breakfast'. No amount of covering him up with anything less than a pillow could stifle the sound. I felt my face turning red as people swivelled in their seats to identify the source of the dinosauric grunts and snuffles.

I am very thankful that neither of my boys met with life-long consequences from certain incidents that could have seriously and even fatally harmed them. Both of them pushed my panic button more than once.

I was changing Daniel's nappy on top of the large chest freezer on the veranda one day and turned to retrieve a fresh diaper from a table approximately a metre behind me. Dan was not yet able to crawl but had not long mastered the roll-over. I thought that since the nappy was so close it would only take one or two seconds to grab it and turn back to finish the task. That was all the time Daniel needed to rotate off the edge of the freezer onto the concrete floor. He cried loudly which common sense told me was probably a good thing as it meant he wasn't unconscious but hardly being up to speed with first aid for a splinter, much less a hard bang to the head on a cement floor, I put him back in his cot. He had just woken from a four-hour nap when the incident occurred and I now know that I probably should have kept him awake and under observation. He slept for another four hours with me nervously checking him every few minutes. When he finally woke up, he was back to himself and I never changed his nappy on the freezer again.

The cot we were using for Daniel came with the Mistake Creek furniture. It was an old-fashioned iron cot with the bars placed further apart than modern cots and I learned why the gaps between cot slats have been narrowed down. Daniel was coming to the end of a-four-hour nap but I wasn't about to disturb him. He would always start making noises to indicate he was ready to get up and, since my 'dog' altercation in Rhodesia all those years ago, I was very much in favour of letting *anything* sleeping lie. However, time passed and still no sound came from Daniel's room. It was Graeme who had come in for lunch and, thankfully not sharing the 'let sleeping dogs lie' policy with me, he opened Daniel's bedroom door. To our horror, the baby had managed to squeeze between the bars of the cot and was suspended by the head, his toes only just touching the floor! His head was too large to fit between the bars and although he suffered no serious effects, he had two significant bruises on either side of his head for a while. We can joke about it now. Dan has a hat size so large that he has to specially order the size that will fit him.

Not to be outdone, Sean had his turn at causing a near cardiac arrest by choking on a piece of banana. He was standing outside the kitchen window prattling on to Karl, the German gardener and Jack-of-all-trades we employed at the time. I was making bread in the kitchen when I

Chapter 14 Mistake Creek Station

heard Karl say something in a voice that held more than a hint of alarm. He was holding Sean and trying to remove something from his mouth. Sean's face was dark red! I rushed out and discovered that Karl had unintentionally pushed the piece of banana further down Sean's throat when he began gagging so there was no possibility of being able to manually hook it out. Turning Sean upside down over my knee, I thumped between his shoulder blades, all the while screaming out for Graeme. He sprinted across from the workshop and took over from me, holding the child over his knee and slapping his back. Sean's face had changed from red to a disturbing purple!

I had read about tracheotomies somewhere in the past. A railway worker had allegedly saved the life of a colleague who was choking on a piece of meat by slipping the blade of a knife into the man's trachea, allowing him to breath. I was on the verge of finding the sharpest kitchen knife available to perform this procedure on our son. I have never been so frightened in my life and the relief I felt when Graeme shouted out 'It's OK. It's come up' can only be described as jellyfish legs, imagining jellyfish having legs. I'm not sure how I managed to stay standing as emotion overwhelmed me! The joy I felt at seeing our little boy's face return to a healthy pink cannot be put in words!

When the Flying Doctor visited later on, I told him of this horrifying incident and asked him what else we could have done if the pseudo-Heimlich manoeuvre hadn't worked.

'Fill a bath with iced water and plunge the victim into it,' he replied. Right! Well, we had a bath but making enough ice to fill it in temperatures of 38 degrees Celsius plus would present an insurmountable problem with only a couple of ordinary-sized freezers on hand and seconds between life and death. I'd have to start sharpening up the kitchen knives! I am so grateful I have never been called on to use this method as a last resort to save a life!

Having been spared from watching our son die by the grace of God, death experiences still cropped up regularly, sometimes in amusing ways. Our Mistake Creek homestead was cooled by ceiling fans and one day my nose, already sensitive to disgusting odours honed by crappy nappies and baby vomit, detected a nasty smell permeating through the house. I can't remember how long we put up with the increasing stench but in due course, fat blowflies began to congregate around one of the fan switches. Removing the switch cover from the wall we located the culprit-turned-victim, a gecko that had become caught in the wiring and fried to death. Geckos were prolific at Mistake Creek and we mostly enjoyed their company but this was not part of the 'mostly enjoyed'. Its carcass was only 6 cm long, if that, but the revolting odour from that tiny cadaver infiltrated the entire residence and took days to be completely gone. A good lesson on the power of little things.

From then on, at the first hint of a similar smell and before the blowflies turned up, Graeme and I studiously

Chapter 14 Mistake Creek Station

tried every evasion tactic to avoid being the one to go from switch to switch to locate the source. We never knew where it would be but when we finally reached the spot, the overpowering aroma almost knocked us off our feet. There was, however an occasion when a vile stench infused our home and the geckos were not to blame.

We had a sink just inside the front door on our veranda where a dirty husband could wash up before entering the house. Outside lay a garden and an outlet where water draining from the sink could flow out into the shrubbery. One day, an Eastern brown snake came slithering up the path and was unfortunate enough to encounter some hostility from our .410 shotgun. Mortally wounded, the reptile crawled into the outlet where it breathed its last. Thinking that was the end of the story, we gave it no more consideration until the house began to reek with a distinctively dead reptilian pong. This time, it was wafting up the drainpipe in the sink. I was happy about this because I could just put the plug in and that would stop the smell from getting into the house, I thought. Having apparently paid no attention to school chemistry lessons, I was about to learn a new thing. The plug kept popping out. No matter how vigorously I jammed it back in, I'd find it exploded back out of the plug hole later on. Apparently, the build-up of gas emanating from the rotting reptile was powerful enough to blow the plug out and I didn't blame the plug for wanting to escape! We were forced to put up with this horrible stink until it finally faded away and I suspect we were thankful henceforth if it was only a fried and over-ripe gecko cadaver that contaminated our house.

While still on the topic of death, it was at Mistake Creek that I came face to face with a human corpse for the second time in my life. Vestey stations not only provided homes and rations for their workers but the worker's old people too and as old folk are inclined to do, one would cash in their chips[32] every so often. This experience was nothing like the peaceful viewing of an old nun in a casket. Rather it was a pulse-searching exercise that gave me the heebie-jeebies that I would make the wrong call on someone who was only comatose. What if I made a ghastly mistake on Mistake Creek and we buried someone who was still alive? I had often pondered on how Mistake Creek Station was so named and prefer the explanation that someone had thought he was travelling up one creek and found it was actually another. Nothing to do with someone being interred alive because of a station manager's incompetent wife!

I soon discovered this was unlikely to happen. Every death had to be reported to the coroner in Darwin and no one could be buried until the coroner gave permission or decided an autopsy was necessary. This time lapse allowed the deceased time to revive if that was what they wanted to do. Quite often, these deaths would occur early in the weekend when the coroner's office was closed. Because we were not aware of the

---

32 Give up the ghost, die

Chapter 14 Mistake Creek Station

correct protocol concerning a deceased 'in waiting', we would simply dig a shallow grave and place the corpse in temporary repose covered with sheets of corrugated iron to protect it from marauding animals. When the coroner returned from his golfing weekend on the Monday, he would view the case and if the deceased was very elderly, gave permission to bury straight away. If the weather was extremely hot as it so often is in the Kimberly, one can understand why graves were never dug to the traditional two metres. Once permission came to bury a two-day old corpse, the deceased's relatives or friends would remove the iron, take a deep breath and shovel in the already-removed dirt as fast as they possibly could without any attempt to deepen the hole.

Another elderly and rather large woman died on a weekend when we were away on our annual leave. Tom was sent to be caretaker and we made the disastrous mistake of not filling him in on the death and burial routine that we had adopted. He was aware that he had to hold the body until Monday but he knew nothing of the shallow grave technique and subsequently left the corpse on the back of the Toyota under a hot tin roof in 40-degree temperatures for two days! Tom laconically informed us on our return that they had to pour the body into the grave. I imagine grave depth was unlikely to be a problem at that point of decay.

While I recognised the need for a coroner's involvement into every death occurring in remote areas, I felt there should be a better way of dealing with corpses that had to wait for a coroner to give the thumbs up or not, particularly if an autopsy might be required. Digging around in the entrails of a cadaver that had been covered for two days with corrugated iron in 38-degree temperatures would put anyone off their lunch. I contacted Darwin and posed the question.

'How are we supposed to preserve these bodies in reasonable condition so they can be autopsied if necessary and burying them isn't so nauseating?' The response was both unexpected and unwelcome.

'Put them in your cold room.'

Every station I know of had a walk-in cold room where perishables were kept and the weekly raw beef supply hung in large chunks along the racks. Even though the deceased was usually wrapped up in their swag cover, there was no way I was going to be navigating around a dead body to retrieve steak for dinner! Off to the shallow grave you go.

We had some wonderful Aboriginal women working for us on Mistake Creek. One of these was my kitchen staff, Ikey. (She can be seen in the photo of the 'cheer squad' when I came home with the biggest baby they had *ever* seen.) When we decided to rope in the services of a shorthorn cow with a bag of milk, Ikey elected to be the milkmaid. I shied away from that job due to past experience.

It was lovely having fresh milk and Ikey did a splendid job but as the season moved along and grass became scarcer, I noticed the milk developing a watery pale bluish tinge.

Chapter 14 Mistake Creek Station

Not knowing much about milk cows, their milk quality and whether or not milk became watery due to lack of proper sustenance, I had to approach Ikey diplomatically. I suspected she was watering the milk down. As honest as the day was long, she admitted she'd been adding water because she thought I would be upset if the milk supply dwindled. Bless her old heart! Consequently, we released the long-suffering milk cow back into the bush and reverted to using Sunshine milk powder in tins.

Ikey and I were chatting one day and I was amazed to hear that both she and Norah, another of our staff, had worked in stock camps as younger women. Ikey had even been one of the mustering team, riding horses and working in dusty yards from dawn to dusk. I inquired of Ikey whether Norah had ridden horses and done any mustering too.

'Nah, missus,' she replied with a cheeky grin. Then putting her hands beneath her swinging breasts, she wriggled them up and down and said, 'Too much jiggle-jiggle.'

I had noticed cobwebs accumulating in the kitchen one day and decided I needed to speak to Ikey about it. It was her job to sweep, mop and keep the webs in control, none of which I was very good at myself but she was paid to do that job.

'Hey Ikey,' I said, finding her with a broom in her hand industriously sweeping the kitchen floor.

'Yeah Missus?'

'You need to sweep the spiders on the ceiling. There's a lot of them, aren't there?' Ikey looked at me, puzzled.

'I nebber see 'im spider, missus,' she said

'Here,' I replied, taking hold of her broom. Reaching up, I touched a spider web and, as Daddy long-legs spiders are inclined to do, the creature quivered vigorously, either to send a strong message to the intruder to get lost or from extreme excitement at the humungous dinner that just landed in its pantry.

'Aaah!' cried Ikey with great delight. 'I can see 'im when 'e move, Missus.' I can't remember if the spider web issue improved after that but knowing Ikey, she would have done her best to please.

Chapter 15

When the rivers run

The Negri River ran past the Mistake Creek homestead a short walk's distance away and we spent many delightful hours filling sugar bags with succulent black bream. The Duncan Highway ran past the homestead less than a kilometre away and where the road crossed the Negri about 10 km further on was the best place to fish, especially after the river had flooded. In these events, the fish would be washed over the crossing into a deep hole, a little stunned and disorientated. When the water cleared, one could sit on the crossing and literally pick their fishy target, drop the line as close to it as possible and … it didn't really matter if one caught the target or not. Anything that took the bait was 'a keeper' (not that we had size restrictions back then or we didn't know about them).

The Negri is a large river and flooded most years,

washing out the road crossing and blocking anyone traveling on the Duncan Highway from reaching stations further on, or Kununurra and the highway to southern states. Fortunately, there was a natural crossing just behind the Aboriginal quarters that we were able to navigate in four-wheel drives, However, one never headed off to town after the Negri had flooded without ensuring rivers further along were crossable. If the Negri came down, it was very likely others had too. Every year, a patch-up job was done on the Negri crossing because Council never could muster sufficient funds to build a proper bridge. Perhaps they knew even then the Duncan would one day be downgraded from a highway to a road so 'don't waste any money there.'

The Negri was privy to many fun times and one almost tragedy. Son Daniel was washed away when our attention was elsewhere and thankfully, it was Sean who yelled out because Daniel didn't make a sound. He was only crawling and wouldn't have understood what was happening to him. Sean had rushed to save his brother and both were being carried by the flow towards a bend in the river. Had he not alerted us, they would both have been swept around the bend and possibly drowned before we found them.

During one wet season when the road crossing had been destroyed again, the Bell family from Ord River Station decided to take their annual leave. There was only one way for them to cross the Negri and the owner of the little rowboat was a man named, of all things, Jimmy Roe. Jimmy

Chapter 15 When the rivers run

offered the use of his boat to transport the Bells and their luggage across the Negri to a vehicle waiting on the other side.

My heart was in my mouth as I witnessed the strong current grasp the little boat in its watery clutches and try to sweep it away while Jimmy rowed energetically. Jimmy won the battle and the boat eventually pulled into the bank on the other side. Graeme, who had gone along to help with the luggage, knew the spot where the vessel had beached and stepped out to secure it. What he didn't know was the flood had gouged away that part of the bank, leaving a sheer drop of about two and half metres. Graeme sunk like a stone. His hat remained floating on top of the water and, being one of his most precious possessions, he rocketed back to the surface in time to retrieve it before it was swept away. We onlookers couldn't stop laughing at the spectacle before us but restrained ourselves until we were certain of his safety.

I also have memories of the time we had gone to town to pick up a new worker and came back to find the Negri flooded. Graeme stripped down to his jocks and swum to the other side to bring back the bulldozer. The heavy machine lumbered across the river without a flinch and the blokes hooked the Toyota on behind. I quickly scrambled up on the dozer with Graeme as flooded rivers made me extremely nervous. Alan, one of our workers, got into the driver's seat of the Toyota and into the river we went. Water surged up over the floor of the dozer around our ankles and when I looked behind to see how Alan was faring, I had to suppress a smile. The Toyota was actually floating with water rushing through the cabin up to his midriff. He had a white-knuckled chokehold on the steering wheel while the vehicle bobbed along behind the heavy machine. Even though I knew the strong currents wouldn't shift the dozer and Alan wasn't going anywhere in a hurry, I still hoped I'd never have to go through anything as nerve-wracking as that again.

We were saddened when we visited the Negri River several years ago to find the river's profile fundamentally changed. Due to constant burning of vegetation in the name of 'carbon credits', there is nothing to slow the flooding waters. The banks have been gouged out and the back route from Mistake Creek homestead was now a three-and-a-half-metre sheer drop. Tonnes of silt had washed down and banked up at the crossing and no doubt there will be much more until the lunacy ceases. So many hectares have been scorched by fire year upon year and not a bird can be heard in those places anymore.

The Behn River was another hindrance during flood season on the Duncan Highway. Nowhere near as wide as the Negri, it was steep and deep and I had the misfortune of being held up on its banks one day while it made up its mind to become crossable.

Not long after we had settled in at Mistake Creek, I received a telegram from Camille of Auvergne Station asking if I wanted to take ownership of an eight-year-old

Chapter 15 When the rivers run

ex-racehorse with the registered name of Square Deal. We nicknamed him 'Hat Rack', partially due to my first painful experience as his owner.

I set off in Graeme's ute to pick him up with home-made horse float in tow. There was to be a party at Mistake Creek that night so I wasted no time but Camille commented on the clouds while I was loading the horse and said they reminded her of the last cyclone they had experienced. I fervently hoped she was wrong but when I reached the Behn River, it was flooded. Not so much for me to think it *might* be crossable since 'if it's flooded, forget it' didn't exist back then. However, prudence compelled me to wait for a while. I stuck a stick in the mud at the water's edge so I could gauge whether it was falling and by how much but time was moving on and I was impatient to get home before dark. Just as I was arguing with my common sense to allow me to make an attempt, a vehicle much smaller than mine entered the river from the opposite bank and crossed over to my side without incident. Nothing like a tie-breaker when arguing with oneself so in I drove.

I reached the middle of the river before water doused the plugs and the vehicle stalled. It refused to start again and I didn't want to flatten the battery so I gingerly stepped into the flow, lowered the back of the horse float and reversed Hat Rack into the water. With just a bridle and no saddle, I scrambled onto his back and we set off into Rosewood Station for help.

Hat Rack's spine was sharp at the beginning and a samurai sword at the end of approximately 12 km. I was never so pleased to see men hop into a station four-wheel drive and head off to rescue my ute and float. I realised too late that I should have asked to borrow a saddle but I hadn't and another 12 km rubbing back and forth on Hat Rack's vertebrae removed a substantial portion of skin from my buttocks.

When I reached the Behn, my vehicle and float had been hauled up onto the opposite bank and the men had managed to get it started again. Hat Rack and I waded across to join them. As I thanked them profusely, they may have wondered at the pained expression on my face but I wasn't about to explain and neither did they ask.

Hatrack and I wait at the Behn river prior to being stuck in the middle.

Chapter 15 When the rivers run

Given the state of the rivers, I had expected to spend the night at Spring Creek. To my dismay, I found that everyone had gone to Mistake Creek for the party so Hat Rack and I trundled on. My plan was to stop at the Negri River and wait for Graeme to come looking for me but the RB creek pulled me up first. I possibly could have crossed this current but my nerves were frayed and raw as my posterior by this time and I simply didn't have the courage to try. At almost the same time I reached this decision, a Land Rover arrived and crossed over the RB to my side. It was my beloved and the relief I felt was so intense, I cried like a baby! Graeme drove the ute and horse float the rest of the way while I took charge of the Land Rover, pulling him out of boggy patches on a couple of occasions. Finally arriving at the Negri River, we left Hat Rack in one of the night horse paddocks, picked out the suitcases of clothes we wanted and waded through the fast-running current, leaving the vehicles on the opposite bank.

After tramping across almost a kilometre of paddock and bush I didn't much feel like joining the party. All I wanted to do was have a soothing hot shower and fall face-first flat on my bed. The party was in full swing and instead of disappearing into the shadows, I forced a brave face and gingerly sat down. I chose the painful option to be sociable because one didn't get to do very much of that on remote stations and it could be a long time between drinks.

While it's true social events were few and far between in

the Kimberly, one yearly event was high on the list of 'must do' functions. The Negri Picnic racecourse was located only a few kilometres away from Nicholson Station and sported a four-day event every year. Station horses were trained for two days of racing, all grass-fed while stockmen chose their favourite horses for two days of rodeo, camp drafting and barrel racing. Stations from hundreds of kilometres around participated, camping around the venue and engaging in a great deal of boozing and merriment.

One of these Picnic race meetings at Negri was filled with a great deal more activity than just racing and rodeoing, I'm sure most of it fuelled by superfluous grog consumption. The meeting kicked off with a riot between the white and Indigenous stockmen, allegedly spawned a few weeks earlier when one of the Aboriginal men who had just been released from prison was allegedly refused a job on Wave Hill Station. When Ralph, the manager of Wave Hill, who knew and identified the man as a stirrer refused him a job, the man apparently hit Ralph. A young white stockman who witnessed the altercation intervened and the riot that began at the Negri Picnic races was reportedly a continuation of that episode. The Aboriginal man at the centre of the dispute and his mates allegedly tracked down the white stockman and the debacle escalated. Big sticks and knives came out, a car was stoned and what seemed to be the entire police force from Halls Creek were deployed and flown to the scene to restore the peace. Once they arrived, an uneasy law and

Chapter 15 When the rivers run

order prevailed but apart from the car that had sustained damage from having rocks hurled at it, a young stockman had to have his cheek or eye stitched, and another young fellow sustained a broken jaw, or what was thought to be one. Time revealed that it wasn't broken but swelled almost to the size of a football. It was all bad news and reports did the rounds that quite a few of the whites were almost in tears with fright. One young bloke we brought over from Nutwood had about twenty Aboriginal men chasing him up the racecourse straight past the grandstand with sticks and knives. It goes without saying that he must have broken the one-kilometre dash since he managed to stay ahead of the baying mob.[33]

When people weren't mingling or running hell for leather in front of an angry crowd, they worked on training their horses. One of the events on the racing card was the Ladies Race. We ladies would be mounted up on a station racehorse and hopefully, (preferably) get the horse past the finishing post. There was a gap or gateway in the rails up the straight about a hundred metres short of the winning post that led to the rodeo arena. When training her horse, Jenny, a bookkeeper from a neighbouring station, failed to drive her steed past the winning post, choosing instead to stop at the gate and ride into the rodeo arena. None of us actually witnessed this happening so the allegation may not

---

33 We had forgotten all about this incident and retrieved the information from the letters I wrote to my brother Andy at the time of the event. Then the memory flooded back!

be correct, but that deduction was difficult to ignore. The starter dropped his flag and we surged forward in a wave. I had a good horse under me but Jenny's was faster and led the field by a couple of lengths. No matter how hard my horse tried to catch them it looked certain Jenny would win. Just as I was reconciling myself to second place, her horse suddenly lunged sideways through the gap and I found myself in the lead. Confused, I began to pull up but shouts from the spectators urged me to keep going. We held on to win the race by an uncomfortably slender margin, the only Ladies Race I remember winning and I can still remember the trophy; a hair dryer.

There was one other occasion the Behn stopped us. Graeme and I were on our way to take up a position on Spring Creek Station with Sean still in utero. The Behn was well up, so we rolled our swags out and prepared to wait it out since we drove a Holden station wagon, low to the ground and only two-wheel drive. The mosquitos were so bad, neither of us slept. Graeme managed to pass time proving his hunting skills by catching a young fresh-water crocodile but we were eventually able to cross the Behn sometime in the middle of the night. We agreed to continue to Spring Creek but hit a rock in the road in the dark and punctured our sump. Graeme managed to catch the oil in the baby's pot and walked to Spring Creek with the ruptured sump while I curled up on the road beside the vehicle.

It astounds me the number of people in these populated

Chapter 15 When the rivers run

areas who lose their lives trying to drive across flooded streams and rivers. I don't remember ever hearing of similar tragedies in the Kimberley and am ever grateful for either our good luck, a lot more 'horse sense' than seems to prevail these days or a superbly diligent guardian angel!

Chapter 16

Bull catching on the Turner

We spent three happy years at Mistake Creek but like all good things do, they came to an end. The company was becoming increasingly difficult to deal with as its hierarchy, encapsulated in glass offices somewhere in the middle of Sydney, made decisions about how a remote cattle station ought to operate without knowing the first thing about it. Instead of trying to purchase the same model lighting plant for all their stations at what would have surely been a heavily discounted price, every property had a different breed of generator. This made part-swapping impossible. It meant a broken-down power plant would remain down for several weeks while new parts were ordered from Perth or Sydney instead of perhaps finding a spare part on another Vestey station.

Chapter 16 Bull catching on the Turner

Along the same lines, the company couldn't afford to provide us with a second-hand body truck and the use of a bulldozer to doze a decent track to the back end of the property which was teeming with cleanskin bulls. These wild bovines caused havoc during mustering, breaking through the ranks and leading the rest of the cattle back into the bush after an expensive helicopter had spent two hours bringing them together. Since horsemen couldn't hold them, we needed a truck to transport them securely back to the station yards where they could be properly processed, castrated and dehorned ready for the bullock paddock. But for the want of a passable road, this couldn't be carried out so approximately eighty bulls were destroyed and left to rot.

On being shown the carnage caused by the company's lack of sensible fiscal policy (as we thought of it), the Pastoral Inspector Ces reflected for a moment.

'Well, I suppose they're better off where they are,' he said. The money eighty head of cleanskin bulls could have brought into the company's coffers would have been more than adequate to buy a bulldozer and body truck.

We had friends from Alice Springs visiting us for a weekend and I came down with what I thought was a tummy bug. Never having experienced morning sickness, I didn't give thought to the possibility I might be pregnant. Time always tells in the end though and our daughter Megan was on her way. It wasn't very long after this revelation that the Ord River Station manager alerted us to a West Australian government advertisement seeking a bull catcher to help clean up the cattle on Turner River Station approximately two hours away on what was little more than a goat track. Graeme pricked up his ears and after we discussed the possibility of surviving life without the Vestey company's regular pay cheques, we chose to bite the bullet and apply. What was there to lose?

Before we knew if our application had been received much less pondered upon, we approached a bank for a loan that would purchase the equipment we required for such an enterprise. Providentially, the caravan we needed was situated on Nelson Springs next door and happened to be for sale, while an eight-ton Bedford truck squatted in our yard, owned by Cam from Adelaide. Cam had been excavating for diamonds and was responsible for finding some of the first diamonds in the area, which eventually led to the Argyle Diamond mine. He had completed his mission and sold us the old truck, relieving himself of having to take it back to Adelaide. The short-wheel-base Toyota that would be converted into a 'catcher' was sourced from Brisbane when we were down for the Christmas break, along with a long-wheel-base Toyota that would serve as our town car. We drove them 4,000-plus km back to Ord River Station where Graeme set about transforming the catcher and making portable panels to erect a holding yard for the bulls — when and if we ever caught any.

The WA government eventually accepted our submission

Chapter 16 Bull catching on the Turner

for the contract and we embarked on the onerous task of moving our now fairly substantial plant onto Turner River Station. This property had belonged to Vestey until it was reclaimed by the West Australian government as catchment for the Ord River Dam. It had not been operational for years, hence the countless numbers of cleanskin cattle that never saw a human being other than old Mick. Mick was a retired drover and camped at Turner River with his Aboriginal wife.

Launching out into business on our own was intimidating. Having lived for so long under the protective umbrella of the Vestey company with regular weekly wages, I spent wakeful nights wondering if we could really succeed in this venture. Oh, me of little faith! When Graeme sets his jaw, failure is never an option and so we were committed; we christened our enterprise 'Love-a-bull Catchers'. That name was easily remembered and even though we only saw Darwin businesses we purchased our seasonal stores from once a year, they never forgot 'Love-a-bull Catchers'.

By the time we began to catch bulls, our new baby was making itself apparent. Fortunately, one of our stockmen from Mistake Creek came with us and we employed him to drive the pick-up truck so I was left to cook the meals, manage our camp and keep an eye on two little boys. The camp consisted of our caravan butted up against an old shed that gave extra space where the boys would sleep. The toilet facility eventually followed; a pit dug in the ground with a seat constructed out of a 200 litre metal drum with a hole carved

Love-a-bull Catchers mascot.

out of the top. This was a great improvement to going behind the bushes for the daily constitutional, especially for me as squatting in my cumbersome state was fraught with potential mishaps. The downside was that, like all out-houses, this bush loo became home to a variety of crawly creatures, and flies by the tonne. The fact it was only surrounded by hessian for privacy and had no roof may have dissuaded the slithery critters from making their homes in it and I was grateful for that. Redback spiders were the only poisonous living things one had to look out for before sitting down.

Every so often, when the flies in and around the dunny became too prolific and the smell became intolerable, Graeme would mix petrol and diesel together, throw it into the pit and follow it up with a lit match. Depending on the

Chapter 16 Bull catching on the Turner

diesel/petrol ratio, there would be a satisfying explosion come from the guts of the dunny and clouds of flies and their maggot offspring would be blown skywards into extinction. This procedure also helped with the odour.

I arrived back at camp one morning oblivious to the fact that Graeme had just completed his housekeeping in the dunny and he wasn't there to warn me. If I were a perceptive person, I would undoubtedly have worked it out for myself but I'm not, so I didn't. It's not difficult to imagine that a fiery explosion in a hole under a steel 200 litre drum could make that drum very hot and imagination became reality for me on this day as I rushed to the dunny and sat down.

I've never been a fast mover. As a little kid in a foot race, a strange kind of 'friend' informed my mother that I looked like a fly drowning in treacle ... and there I was, thinking I was really *moving!* On this day, it took me about three seconds to move very fast indeed as I launched myself skyward! And that's when I was thankful again — no roof on the dunny! My 'sit upon' had the sensation of being sunburnt for several days and served as an effective reminder to tentatively touch the dunny seat before using it.

Our bath was the Turner River that flowed a couple of metres away from the caravan. As Daniel appeared want to do, he came close to drowning in that river as well and again thanks to big brother Sean, we retrieved him safely.

We had a portable power plant that kept our fridges

cold and motivated the old wringer washing machine we'd managed to find so we lacked for nothing of any importance. Sometimes we would hang our butter in a wet hessian bag in a shady breeze-way and our fresh meat was suspended in the open air overnight and stored under gum leaves beneath the caravan during the day. Transmitter radios kept us in touch with the outside world and enabled us to order stock as required.

We loved the bull-catching life and so did the boys. Sean was enrolled in School of the Air so some of our time was designated to doing 'school' through Derby. Due to the remote location and mountains in the way, radio contact with Derby was abysmal and Sean and I both struggled. I knew we would have to move to civilisation eventually if we didn't want our children to be morons but that was too far in the future to ruin the enjoyment of each day in this idyllic setting.

Our truck driver's wife was heavily pregnant with their third child and had made up her mind that she would have the baby in their caravan, which was parked close to the bull yards. We were uneasy about this even though she had already successfully had one home birth. The closest airstrip for the Flying Doctor was at Ord River Station over two bumpy hours away on a rough track so anyone caught up in an emergency was going to need a lot of luck. At my insistence I drove Judy to one medical check-up with the Flying Doctor when he visited Ord River Station, lecturing her all the way

Chapter 16 Bull catching on the Turner

on the possible dangers of something going wrong with her birth on Turner River Station. Even the doctor told her firmly that if she got into trouble, she would have to pay for the Flying Doctor to pick her up — if she made it that far. All this fell on deaf ears and Judy breezily produced her third baby in the caravan without incident. I was relieved because I didn't relish the thought of having to play 'midwife' when up to that point I hadn't even pulled a calf.

At some point after all this excitement, our truckie and his family left us and we were minus a truck driver. There was no one but me to fill the gap until another could be found, which I was happy to do and I trundled after the catcher with the two boys in the cabin with me, contented to wait under a tree until I was summoned. My stomach had enlarged considerably by this time and my feet were rarely seen except when bathing in the river. Climbing into the truck presented a challenge — getting down even more so. My bulk prohibited me from turning around and dismounting backwards so I was left with no alternative but to jump to the ground. There were times when I felt as if the baby was going to keep on going when my feet hit terra firma but it hung in there, obviously well cushioned.

'Tough little beggar,' I thought. We have often joked that Megan was supposed to be a boy but I 'shook the pecker off her.'

While Graeme operated the bull catcher and was responsible for knocking over and restraining the bulls with leather straps, I was to wait some distance away until he'd caught everything in the area. He would then call me up on the two-way radio and I'd sidle the truck up close to the bulls so they could be loaded. The loading was performed by the use of a pulley above the dropgate of the crate and steel cable which would be looped around the bulls' horns. From the horns, the cable was threaded through the pully and back down to the catcher. At this point I would jump out of the truck, (waking the baby again), and take command of the catcher. After the cable was secured to both bull and catcher, I drove slowly away, hauling the animal up the dropped slide gate. Halfway up the ramp, the leg straps were removed

The conquered and the conqueror, Turner River station.

Chapter 16   Bull catching on the Turner

and the animal was pulled the rest of the way into the truck. He was then secured to the crate with a rope around the horns to prevent him from fighting other bulls already on board.

Occasionally, a bull's leg might be dislocated in the course of being rolled. This was seldom evident until he attempted to get to his feet in the back of the truck. He wouldn't go to Wyndham this time and once the rope around his horns was released, he would slide down the drop-gate and bolt for the bush. At least that's what they usually did.

I was standing at the door of the truck on one occasion seeing to the two boys in the cab. Heavily pregnant with our daughter, climbing up and down out of the cab of an eight-ton truck many times a day had made me fit. But I was 'fat' and while the fitness was a good thing here, the fat bit was about to present me with a problem.

Unbeknownst to me, a bull with a dislocated leg had been released from captivity but instead of bolting into the bush as they usually do, this one decided to seek revenge. He didn't give the catcher a second glance, having already been humiliated by its superior size and weight but there was a soft pink target standing at the truck door that would do instead. I was blissfully unaware of the malicious intent running through the animal's cranium.

Fortunately for me, my peripheral vision saw it coming straight at me up the side of the truck so I nippily zipped (waddled) around the snubby nose of the vehicle to the other-side door. I was certain the animal would head for the trees *as they usually do,* but I didn't account for a rebellious mean streak. Instead, a loud and snotty snort closely followed by a bull's nose appeared around the front of the truck a metre from my shoulder. I was a little perturbed by this but thought I could just scramble under the truck and be safe. This is where the 'fat' bit betrayed me. I was unable to bend down low enough and quickly enough to save myself that way so was compelled to leg it around the back of the truck. This time I was very much on my guard and … uh oh! Around he came again!

The bull pursued me around the truck two and a half times before my gallant husband rescued me. Like me, he thought the bull would be in such a hurry to escape, it would rush on past the nose of the truck and disappear into the bush (because that's what they *usually* do) so he sat back to enjoy the show. I didn't see him laughing but he assured me later, with tears in his eyes and a smile wider than Sydney Harbour Bridge, that he couldn't help it! Thankfully, he eventually appreciated that I really did need assistance and, in the safety of the catcher he bulldozed the animal, pushing it away from the truck and into the bush.

Prior to our move to Turner River to take up our bull catching contract, we were gifted a nanny goat. A meaner, more devilish-looking creature I'd never come across, in addition to which she was twelve years old and cranky! One always had to keep at least one eye but preferably two

Chapter 16 Bull catching on the Turner

firmly fixed on her if she were anywhere in range because to be complacent was perilous! Anyone was fair game to this old 'sweetheart' and the only reason we kept her was because she was 'expecting' a little goat we could eventually use for rations.

I'll call her 'Goat' because any of the other names I thought up for her are unprintable and 'Nanny' was too benign for the likes of her. We took her down to our Turner River camp along with our ex-Mistake Creek horse Imp and she seemed happy enough to roam freely while keeping close to camp. Her belly expanded quickly until one night, she produced a little boy kid. We then broke the old biddy in to be milked and it was good to enjoy fresh milk, powdered milk being the only milk we could keep in a cupboard that didn't go off. Sometimes Goat would find a clump of delectable weed which contaminated her milk with a not so delectable flavour. It was still consumable but only just.

Goat made the mistake of wandering into our supply store, which was set up on wooden pallets outside the van. It would have been alright if she had kept wandering and left it alone but being a daughter of the devil, she determined to run a taste test on everything she could get into. Flour bags were broken open, Golden Syrup tins with the lids off (and I'll never know how she accomplished that,) all mixed together in a ghastly mess and spread from one side of the store of provisions to the other. Lunging for the straw broom, I sent her skittering down the bank with a hearty whack on the rump and hope in my heart that she would be smart enough to double-think before trying again. All she did was double-check that no one was around and I came home the next time to find her fetlock-deep in goodies again.

    I don't lose my temper easily but something like an old-fashioned camera flash popped in my brain. Goat was going to die! Putting a rope around her horns, I hitched her up to the back of the truck and loaded up the .22 rifle. To say my skills with a gun are border-line dangerous is a nice way of saying I'm flat out hitting a barn from 10 m but will most likely hit everything else so here was a volatile situation. Of course, the old felon wasn't going to stand still for me and I was so mad at her, I was shaking and couldn't take a steady aim. Furious as I was with the bearded fiend, I was appalled at the thought of misfiring and mortally wounding her. My compassion for her beggars belief, but I was much more concerned for my old dog Mac who was resting peacefully under the truck. Graeme arrived home to find us both swinging from side to side, Goat trying to escape and me trying to keep up with her. He couldn't restrain his laughter and relieved me of being executioner that day. Goat was not so fortunate and we were left with the kid.

    Christmas holidays were looming so we butchered the kid and dropped it off at Ord River Station for them to enjoy. We heard later the power plant broke down the day after our delivery and all perishable goods went off and had to

Chapter 16 Bull catching on the Turner

be thrown out, including the kid. So much effort, not to mention expense and stress for so little return.

Our baby was due to arrive during this holiday so she would be born in the Kingaroy hospital. The due date came and went, then another day, and another. In the meantime, I had become engrossed in a three-part mini-series on television about Ned Kelly and I was hoping the baby wouldn't come until I had finished watching the series. On the night of the final episode, symptoms began to manifest themselves — little contractions placed wide apart. They weren't painful at all so I continued to watch Ned Kelly with hand on belly in monitoring mode.

It was after 11 pm when Ned Kelly gave up his ghost that I suggested to Graeme it might be wise to ring the hospital. Based on the information I gave them, they called me in. Grabbing my hospital bag, Graeme drove me sedately into Kingaroy, some 20 km from his parents' farm where we were staying.

On arrival at the maternity section, I was whisked away to be examined.

'Oh my! You're 5 cm dilated. We'd better get you to the labour ward right now.'

I had felt no pain at all and was lying on the labour ward bed thinking perhaps we had jumped the gun when a searing, indescribably agonising bolt of pain ripped through my abdomen. It scared the living daylights out of me because I knew what labour pains felt like now and this was *nothing* like that. It subsided and I thought I'd hang on and see what would happen next. I wasn't disappointed. Far worse than the first pain, I pressed the buzzer. Within seconds, the nurse was with me and I was in full push mode.

'Breathe,' she commanded. 'Try not to push yet, it's too soon' but her advice didn't make it anywhere near my brain's centre of reason and within seconds, our daughter burst into the world after only two 'grunts through the bottom'. She was caught by expert hands before taking a nose-dive off the end of the bed and I met our new baby, daughter Megan Joanne.

Many have said they wished they had experienced similar 'easy' births and it was undeniably 'easy' compared to a lot. However, when a baby literally blasts from the body like a human cannonball, it generally causes damage. Enter the doctor who had been called to deliver the baby but arrived after the fact dressed in a red track suit, swinging a surgical mask on the end of his finger. The job of stitching things together was left to him and what a scene that must have been!

Feet in stirrups and knees apart, the doctor's head looked not unlike a cow about to be caught in a head bale. Industriously, he plied his needle and twine like a seasoned seamstress, stitching me back together while his tongue ran laps around his lips and I had to stop myself from laughing. Wouldn't want to cause a slip, would I? I was also dealing with cramps so laughing was off the table at the time. Job

Chapter 16 Bull catching on the Turner

done and back in my hospital bed, an ice bag was brought to me for 'you know where'. That was the pinnacle of the entire experience. Along came a rubber glove that had been filled with water and frozen solid! After all that I'd been through I was about to be goosed[34] by a glove!

Finally released from hospital, Graeme took me back to the farm and the battles began. Like her brothers before her, Megan suffered from an over-supply of very fast flowing milk and suffered terribly with colic. I used to sit with her in the lounge room into all hours of the night in efforts to not wake the rest of the house until Graeme decided he'd had enough. Making sure the baby was comfortable and dry in her bassinet, he took me by the hand, closed the door on our daughter and led me to bed. Improvement in her colicky situation followed more quickly than it had with the boys as I eventually made Megan suck up-hill. Not the most comfortable way to breastfeed, it put a stop to her being drowned by a superfluous 'let down' and the tummy pains subsided.

Back on Turner River and with new truck driver Glen and his wife and family added to our team, I reverted back to being 'house wife' with meals to prepare and three children to keep in line. Being too small to wash in the river, Megan was bathed in a cut-off twenty litre drum, which was perfect for the task. Sean and I continued to 'waste' many hours trying to cope with a School of the Air that we could

---

34 To press or take hold of someone's bottom.

Megan bathing in a cut-off drum on Turner River station.

hear but who couldn't hear us and I watched my eldest lose confidence and become sad because he was never picked by the teacher when he knew answers to questions. He was due to start school proper the following year. The time to leave was rapidly approaching.

What twelve years working for Vestey had not been able to achieve, two years of bull-catching allowed us to accumulate sufficient funds to place a deposit on our own farm, which we purchased after our first year of catching. I knew Graeme would have loved to continue on but I think he understood that schooling up in this 'middle of nowhere' place was harrowing for both teacher/mother and her student so it was with both excitement and sadness that we began preparations to move back to the South Burnett.

Chapter 16   Bull catching on the Turner

The convoy heading back to the South Burnett in Queensland.

Glen and Maree were keen to take over our bull-catching plant and continue on so it was convenient for us to be able to sell the Toyotas, old Bedford truck and portable yards to them. We had sourced another truck from Townsville on which our goods, chattels and two horses, the second of which we purchased just prior to leaving, were to be loaded and transported south. We had also replaced the long-wheel-base Toyota with a yellow Toyota Hilux utility. Mac the mutt would ride on the back of that, along with whatever wouldn't fit in the truck. Tim and Joc from Helen Springs were migrating south at the same time so we joined forces and travelled to our new lives together. Graeme drove the truck while I drove the Hilux as a sort of support vehicle in case one of the trucks had mechanical trouble.

We spent two years catching bulls on Turner River. Each

day was a picnic as we packed children and lunches and set off for the day's catching. Often, we'd pull over beside a beautiful waterhole or creek where the children could swim and play while we ate lunch before continuing the day's catching. Sundays were always days off and we would have 'church' in one of so many lovely locations that made us very aware of, and appreciative to, the Creator of all things. Always spent on the banks of a river and, in one rather unnerving incident, swimming under the gaze of multiple fresh-water crocodiles, we rested and prepared for a new week of matching wits against creatures accomplished in the art of evasion. It was, indeed, paradise.

CHAPTER 17

Back to civilisation

Our primary purpose for going bull-catching was to gather sufficient funds to buy a farm back in Queensland where Graeme originated. In two seasons we accomplished that goal and it was with heavy hearts that we left the Kimberley to start a new life on our 260-hectare block at Kinleymore near Proston.

It was probably a few years before the yearning for wide-open and amazingly beautiful spaces settled down to a barely tolerable ache. Graeme felt it much more than I as he always says the best years of his life were spent in packhorse camps on Spring Creek. Every March when there was a distinctly autumnal chill in the air, Graeme would think about mustering the horses ready for the stock camp but we only had two horses. Both had been brought down with us and mustering them just didn't fill the void. Like an aged piker bullock waiting for the wire to break so he can return to the wild country, Graeme said he would often find himself restlessly 'pacing the back fences' and sniffing the neighbour's cooking on the wind. Adjusting to a farm half the size of the horse paddock on most Kimberly and Northern Territory stations felt akin to squashing into *really* tight jeans.

Seven years on the Kinleymore farm was plagued with drought and exorbitantly high interest rates of nineteen and a half per cent when Paul Keating was Prime Minister. In order to make ends meet, Graeme found work on the Boondooma Dam construction site as well as breaking in horses and growing a large vegetable garden. Our meagre income wasn't sufficient to buy fruit but we were able to barter our vegetables in exchange for fruit at the local fruit shop in Proston, for which we were grateful.

We had a share farmer growing crops on our land since we were definitely not 'agricultural' people and the proceeds from those crops were divvied up between us. Errol did a fantastic job but consistently bad seasons saw a majority of the crops fail. This eventually wore us out but getting to that point where we both wore out together and found ourselves on the same page didn't come easily. When one of us felt a strong inclination to sell the property and move to a more favourable climatic location, the other was up-beat and optimistic that things were going to improve and wanted to stick it out. This see-saw continued for a year or two until we happened to park outside a Real Estate agent in Murgon

Chapter 17 Back to civilisation

one day. As if taken from a script and choreographed, we looked at each other and said, 'Let's list the farm.'

Several viewers came to inspect over a period of nearly two years but without success until quite suddenly, our patience was rewarded when people who lived almost spitting distance away came to look. Not long after, they returned with their parents for another look and following close on the heels of that came an offer we weren't about to refuse. Almost immediately, we were only two weeks or so off being homeless and Graeme rushed away in a cloud of dust to find us a new home.

Real Estate Agents in Kingaroy at that time seemed largely apathetic about doing much more than handing Graeme a list of available acreage in the Tingoora area where he set his heart on going if at all possible. We need not have been concerned though as the first farm on the list that he visited was exactly what he was searching for. He immediately spoke to the owner, making sure he was aware of our interest and asking if he would hold out until Graeme had a chance to bring me for a look? Pat was happy with that arrangement and we ultimately purchased his property without using an agent.

Located walking distance from Tingoora township and divided into four titles, we have been on this beautiful farm for thirty-four years now and hope never to have to leave it, no matter how unrealistic that dream might be. The farm had been solely used for dairying and cropping in the past. It had no fences to speak of when we moved in except derelict fences on either side of the two gullies that traverse the property. No trees either apart from what grew naturally in the water courses, a large portion of which comprised of wall-to-wall Groundsel over three and a half metres high. There was also a heavy infestation of Noogoora burr which formed a handy diversion for naughty kids!

'Get out there and pull Noogoora burr for an hour' became a mantra in our house for many years and evoked memories of my bed stripping days at school. The prolific box thorn and Thorn Apple or stramonium also took up a great deal of time and effort and even though the farm is clean of all those pests now, Graeme habitually wanders the paddocks with a mattock or hoe to ensure they stay under control. This venture was the beginning of a great deal of blood, sweat and tears and we soon realised how cushy the job of catching feral bulls had been!

Over the ensuing years, the property was divided into paddocks. Post holes had to be dug with a crowbar and shovel as we had no capital to spend on mechanised aids, which were pitifully few. One old blue tractor and a couple of rusty-looking agricultural implements that came with the farm was the full extent of the equipment we had to pull the property into shape. The tractor was eventually upgraded to another bigger, marginally less geriatric red tractor (please don't ask me to name the make and model but I *think* it's an International) and other farm implements

Chapter 17 Back to civilisation

were added as and when the bank balance permitted.

We have planted thousands of trees and are still planting trees. Graeme puts them in the soil and I help him with the watering. It's seeing the size of these trees now that helps us remember how long we have been here because the years pass as quickly as shadows.

Being all black soil as opposed to the old farm's red porous soil, this is much better cropping country. The weather also seems more reliable for agriculture and we were able to harvest quite a few acres of crops successfully over the years. This phased out as the area built up and spraying crops become more contentious. We planted improved pastures and devoted our enterprise entirely to breeding Limousin Stud cattle, which we had started off at Kinleymore as the Hillsborough Limousin Stud. These cattle have brought us tremendous pleasure and satisfaction both in and out of the show ring and my usual response to the question 'Do you breed Limousins?' is 'Is there any other breed?' Call me biased, I am unashamedly a Limousin fan and Graeme is even more so, having worked with so many liquorice all-sorts in the bovine world throughout his life. However, I still hold a soft spot for the regal Brahman cattle and nostalgically remember my introduction to the world of leading and showing cattle as a child.

We now have eight grandchildren. Sean and Megan both reside in Kingaroy, a twenty-minute drive away from us. Sean has four children and Megan has two. Daniel lives in the United States and has two children.

Having enjoyed what I always thought was great health all my life, I was found to have polycystic kidneys at the age of fifty. Still feeling extremely well, I ignored all this until around Christmas 2020 when I suffered a fractured pelvis.

Graeme had called me up to the shed to help him in the construction of some heavy steel yard corners. My job was to hold them upright while he welded. Unfortunately for me, after lifting the contraption into an upright position for me, he let go before I had a decent hold. I lost my footing and crash-landed on my backside on the hard cement floor with the weight of the steel corner on top of me. I dare say it might have looked funny with me framed by a steel corner, my head poking through the rails but the agony took all the fun out of it, not to mention my breath!

Eventually, I had to go to the general hospital in Toowoomba where the fracture was found. However, this was considered relatively minor when they also discovered my kidneys were only functioning at a low 9 per cent (I don't know why they bothered). Now I am consigned to fronting up to the Kingaroy Hospital Renal Unit for dialysis twice a week ... and I'm one of the lucky ones! Is it a nuisance, you might ask? Yes, but the ten hours I lose having a machine doing its best to equal God's created organs and getting nowhere near it is worthwhile because I now understand that I was probably dying slowly and didn't recognise it.

Chapter 17 Back to civilisation

One of our champion Limousin stud cows.

Like putting a frog in cold water and bringing the water to the boil, the poor old frog gets used to the increasing heat until it's dead. I never was very energetic for almost as long as I can remember but I thought that was just me being lazy and/or getting 'old'. Graeme wouldn't let me drive for long distances as I was inclined to fall asleep at the wheel. Since dialysis, I can drive distances again with confidence — for the most part. Just not after lunch when I'm due for a Nanna nap! I intend to make the most of it before old age finally gets my licence rescinded!

The nurses in the Renal Unit are amazing and tend to spoil their patients. Each time someone celebrates a birthday, they trot out a birthday mud cake and we are showered with little packets of chocolates over Easter and Christmas candies during the festive season.

'Are you diabetic?' is the stock-standard question (because so many on dialysis are).

'No,' is my stock-standard response, 'but you sure seem hell-bent on sending me in that direction.'

They say every cloud has a silvery lining and I've found this to be true most of my life. I tell everyone that dialysis is not all doom and gloom and while it bites a chunk of ten hours out of my life, they come out of the housekeeping allocation. That makes both me and the spiders very happy indeed!

CHAPTER 18

Remarkable reunions

I have mentioned a few people during the course of this journey that I met again many years after losing contact. Their surprise, and sometimes unwelcome, re-appearance in my life showed me that our world is really a small place in the big scheme of things.

The first, and most extraordinary of these reunions happened with Norma. After bidding her farewell in Rhodesia as she headed off on her honeymoon, I wondered if and when we would ever meet again. Little did I know.

Norma and I continued to correspond after I reached Australia although she couldn't be described as a consistent letter-writer. I was usually the one that furnished her with detailed descriptions of my new life, receiving only short replies without much news at all — that is until she told me approximately one year after her wedding that she was in the process of divorcing her husband. Apparently, the marriage had been a disaster and Norma and Brian had quickly grown apart, leaving her wishing she had come to Australia with me as originally planned. Now her letters were telling me she would be coming to Australia but there were emigration problems and she would probably have to go to England first. When Graeme and I went over to Rhodesia for our belated honeymoon, we caught up with Norma and had lunch with her in Salisbury (now Harare). Although I asked about her marriage, she was reluctant to talk about it but left us in no doubt that there would be no reconciliation.

Norma then quietly dropped out of my life altogether until two or three years later when we were managing Mistake Creek Station. A letter arrived to say she had landed in Sydney at last. Almost by return mail (our mail service only ran once a week) I wrote back to the address on her letter but received no response. Nothing unusual about that, I thought and put it all behind me again to get on with life, often wondering what had become of her.

A new station hand was hired for Mistake Creek and Graeme sent me to Kununurra to pick him up off the bus due in from Darwin in the afternoon. It was a long trip into town, roughly two and a half hours of dirt road, and I was happy that Graeme had kept the children home with him. I did some shopping for stores and then went to wait for the bus. It was late — very late and dark was fast approaching.

Chapter 18 Remarkable reunions

Having expected a day trip and totally unprepared for an overnight stay in Kununurra, I resolved to return home. If our man arrived after I'd gone, he would have to find a place to roll out his swag and I would just have to make a trip back the next day to get him.

Not long before reaching the turnoff from the highway back onto the dirt road, I saw the unmistakable lights of a bus approaching me in the dark ahead.

'Blow it,' I thought. 'I'll bet that's the bus and our bloke is on it.' As the bus swished past in the gathering gloom, I swung the Toyota around and screamed off in hot pursuit. Not accustomed to being asked for such a turn of speed, the poor old thing rattled, shuddered and bellowed in protest as the speedometer needle crept past numbers it had never seen in its life! I passed that bus like a demon possessed, putting enough distance between us to allow me to pull over, jump out and flag it down. I have no idea what the bus driver thought but he must have figured he had enough passengers to support him if I was looking for a fight so he parked on the side of the road. The door glided open smoothly with a soft hiss as bus doors do and I asked the surprised driver if our man was on board. He turned round and called out the name of our employee.

'Hello Val.' A soft voice drifted down to me from the front seat behind the driver. I looked into a face I knew but I couldn't remember for the life of me who it was.

'I know you,' I said, 'but I can't remember your name'.

'Norma,' she replied. In the next second it dawned on me who I was staring at and she leapt out of the bus! We hugged and I spluttered something like, 'Have you come to stay with us — a surprise visit?'

'No,' Norma replied. 'I'm actually on a bus trip around Australia.' I gaped at her in speechless surprise, giving a star-like imitation of a dying fish. In the meantime, the man I had come to collect had his baggage in the back of my Toyota and the bus driver was beginning to tap his fingers on the steering wheel. Norma and I quickly exchanged addresses and she re-boarded the bus.

'Goodbye Val,' she said as the doors whispered shut behind her. I waved but it was dark by then and I wasn't able to see her anymore. I watched the taillights of the bus receding up the highway into the Kimberly night and I never saw or heard from Norma again. I wrote to the address she gave me that night the moment I got home but as I had come to expect, there was no reply nor ever has been.

The coincidence of this remarkable reunion still astonishes me because if Norma had been in any other seat than that which she was in, we would have been unable to see each other. Even if she'd been in the window seat of that particular seat, she would have been obscured from my sight. Only two seats had clear visibility out through the door that night — the driver and the aisle seat immediately behind him where Norma sat.

It wasn't too long after we had moved to Tingoora,

Chapter 18 Remarkable reunions

approximately eighteen years after I came to Australia on the P & O liner *Canberra* that I bumped into big John B, one of my shipboard companions and the one who had helped me find my way onto the train for Bowral. We had stopped writing to each other shortly after my arrival at Auvergne and I hadn't heard from him or seen him again. That is until we took cattle down to Farmfest at Toowoomba.

The Limousin stand was set up and Graeme and I took turns looking after it and talking to what we hoped would be prospective bull-buyers. On my return from a walk around the grounds, Graeme told me a bloke from the Simmental stand next door had heard us talking and had come to enquire. He told Graeme that when he heard my voice, he knew immediately who I was and he had come to verify that I was indeed the Val Hames he thought I might be and with whom he had travelled all those years ago. I could hardly believe my eyes! John owned Old Talgai Station breeding Simmental cattle and we spent more than an hour catching up on the years that had so swiftly passed until duty called. He hadn't changed much apart from his nose, which had the appearance of someone who had enjoyed a bit of grog through the years. Otherwise, he was much as I remembered him. I think I saw John once or twice at shows after that but haven't seen him now for a number of years and wonder if he still owns Old Talgai.

Kimble, Jerry and Joan's daughter who had been a very small child when I arrived at Bowral didn't personally turn up in my life again, but rather in a second-hand sort of way. She met up with Andy, Tim and Joc's son, when Andy was flying helicopters in the Kimberley many years after we'd moved down to SE Queensland. It seemed quite odd hearing news of the Vavasours with whom I'd grown up from Tim and Joc, especially since I hadn't heard from any of them since I bumped into Jerry and Joan at the Brunette Downs Races just after Graeme and I became engaged. I would subsequently pass that news on to my brothers on the other side of the world and who also often wondered what the Vavasour clan was up to.

And last, but not least if only for the fact this was the last person I wanted back in my life, Tino popped up like the proverbial bad penny. I'd not heard anything about him since our bitter and final break-up in 1973 and had managed to rid him from my mind for good, I thought. Then one night the phone rang. I can't remember the name but it was an acquaintance from many hundreds of kilometres away asking Graeme if he'd read the latest *Country Life* newspaper.

'Some bloke has put an advertisement in, looking for your wife,' the informant told Graeme. Sure enough, when we bought the paper there was the advertisement asking people who might know my whereabouts to please contact Tino. I felt myself doing my beached fish impersonation yet again, horrified at this perceived invasion back into my life. I felt as if I had swallowed an enormous rock that crashed-landed

Chapter 18 Remarkable reunions

in the pit of my stomach. At least it squashed the butterflies! He was back! He always said he'd find me and here he was, about to do just that. Many calls came in over the next few days and we asked each of the callers not to pass information of my whereabouts back to Tino. In the end, it didn't matter. Not long after the advertisement appeared, I received a lengthy letter from Tino telling me the *Queensland Country Life* paper had given him our address!

To say I was furious isn't an exaggeration. In fact, I was so wild I wrote to QCL advising them of their lack of common sense and privacy consideration and how angry I was with them. I further pointed out that if Tino had been someone with a grudge seeking revenge for something I had or hadn't done, the story might have ended in a tragically different way. Now he knew where I lived and continued to send cards and emails to me. I didn't answer his correspondence to begin with. I grudgingly returned his Christmas greetings and only if I received one from him *and* his lovely wife Olga. It transpired that Olga was a concert pianist and Tino began to send me CDs of her music, most of which I enjoyed. Once again, I found myself in turmoil, scanning the streets wondering if he was going to turn up on my doorstep, feeling unsettled and fearful each time the phone rang.

Tino was a prolific emailer so when his emails suddenly stopped, I felt obliged to ask Olga if he was OK. She informed me he had passed away and it was as if his ghost left my soul and went with him. Finally, I was free. I corresponded with Olga occasionally until she too became abnormally quiet. Since she was a concert pianist, I searched Google to see if I could find any news of her. One lonely little funeral notice popped up stating that she too had passed into the world beyond.

With huge advances in technology and our freedom to travel the world at will, everyone has to face the possibility they might bump into someone they used to know years ago. It appears every time we have travelled, we've been destined to find ourselves sitting next to someone we know that comes from our area or knows someone with whom we are well acquainted. While travelling to England by ship after he finished school, my brother Andrew met a boy whose parents had known my parents in the Argentine! As the saying goes, you can run but you can't hide so it's always best to behave!

CENTURION AND I GO RIDING ...

1 Saddling up

2. I establish supremacy.

3. Warm up!

4. Centurion establishes supremacy

5. Centurion has doubts.

6. Going home

7. And we'll do it again tomorrow!

PART 2

Trail Rides and Picnic Lunches

(As told by Graeme)

INTRODUCTION

When my husband-to-be and I crossed paths in the Kimberley in 1973, the atmosphere sprouted icicles when he gazed at me stonily and made what was possibly the most chauvinistic remark of the century! However, patience and forbearance led to uncovering a truly remarkable individual with a larger-than-life story of his own. Over the years, I have heard him pass on his experiences so many times to so many people, often more than once, and came to one major conclusion. His story should be written.

Unique in so many ways, this past station manager, bull catcher, Chairman and board member of the Queensland Limousin Society, cattle judge at the Brisbane Exhibition, Chairman of the Tick Eradication programme and candidate for the Federal seat of Wide Bay is a man who can do anything he puts his hand to ... except sing ... in tune.

A more talented individual I have yet to meet and when he grins and tells *everybody* that I came more than halfway around the world to improve my genetics I suspect, albeit at a *very* deep subconscious level, perhaps he was right.

Never one to willingly back down from a debate, my 'gene improver' has never been a 'fighter' in the true Aussie sense of the word. Apart from once clipping a young stockman on the ear for giving cheek, he says he won his last fight by a hundred metres and three fences.

'Trail Rides and Picnic Lunches' is Graeme's story. He wrote it in note form and I typed it up for him, smoothing some of the rougher edges off along the way. The credit goes to him. He's lived his life to the fullest extent possible, providing ample fodder for an entertaining yarn around the campfire.

When asked if he will write another book of life after the Kimberley, Graeme says there isn't another book in him. However, thinking of all that he's done since leaving the north and everything he's left out that could have possibly been put in this one, I'm not sure that's true. Age may be a bigger factor in forming that opinion than simply having nothing more to say.

CHAPTER 1

Manbulloo Station

As my age increases, I cast the mind backwards to the past more frequently. If not bewailing how good the old days were and how the country is going to hell in a hand basket, I fondly remember the enjoyment and freedom I experienced in those times. Although I am often guilty of the former, it is the latter that motivated me to write the memories of my youthful days in the Kimberly region of Australia where I roamed for twelve of the happiest years of my life, free of the trappings that eventually accumulated and encumbered me over time. A ute, a swag, a saddle and sometimes a dog, later replaced by my wife, were the sum total of my possessions then and I have often thought it might be pleasant to be free of our current accrual (with the possible exception of the wife) and return to those carefree days.

Since my memories are scattered, recollections will be somewhat scattered reminiscences of experiences on different stations, horses I have known, medical experiences and so on. I like to think that my grandchildren might read about 'Pop's' involvements on the big cattle runs in the north and learn about things they will likely never encounter for themselves such as packhorse camps and broncoing. Technology has overtaken us in gigantic leaps and there would be few, if any stations that utilise those *ancient* methods of stockmanship anymore so those arts will soon be lost in the fog of time and so-called advancement.

Unlike my wife Val, who has written her story for our children from babyhood through to when she met me, my childhood doesn't play a large part in this narrative. I was born into a family of seven children of which I was the third oldest. The first and only daughter arrived about sixteen months later, and although Valmai and I are close mates, I feel I was mostly left to bring myself up while my parents recovered from the shock and accustomed themselves to changing nappies on a girl.

I wasn't about to win accolades from my parents for my academic prowess at school either. I was not partial to sitting still for too long and those hard school benches complete with ink well did nothing to stimulate my enthusiasm. I would often be located in the vegetable garden instead of doing the homework I needed to complete in order to improve my grades and while my parents and teachers

A little stockman in the making.
Back row — Mum, sister Val and Dad.
Front L – R brothers James, John and me.

thought I was intelligent enough to go into the academic classes, I still wonder what I did to give them that idea since I certainly tried every trick in the book to avoid it! Thankfully, 'salvation' came in the form of Stock and

Station Agent Lloyd Murray. He was seeking new recruits and decided he wanted me on his team so on those grounds my parents allowed me to leave school when I completed Grade 10. Thus, with a great sigh of relief, I escaped the so-called halls of academia.

My mother Avey May (known only as May) said I was born in a hurry and have been in one ever since and while I enjoyed working for a stock and station agent, I had energy to burn that wasn't burning in saleyards or auctions. I yearned for more excitement and adventure and having heard about huge northern cattle stations, cattle barons and the exhilaration of dealing with thousands of cattle instead of one or two hundred as the case was, I determined to head north. An old pony club acquaintance happened to be employed on Manbulloo Station so I wrote to him asking for Vestey's Head Office address. In due course, he sent his response with the required information and I wasted not a minute submitting my application to the company. I don't remember the finer details of my being accepted but I received a plane ticket from Brisbane to Katherine and I was on my way. I didn't know I would be away for twelve years but on that note these memories of the best days of my life begin. Some of the names of places and people may not be spelled correctly as they were names I only heard spoken and never saw written.

Manbulloo was the first property I worked on in my youth when I scored a job with Vestey as an eighteen-year-old boy in 1969. I had no idea what to expect, being a month into my

Chapter 1 Manbulloo Station

eighteenth year and inexperienced in the ways of the world but I was ready for whatever lay ahead. Anything had to be an improvement on trudging around saleyards on foot, pushing cattle from pens to scales. Remembering Mum's description of being 'born in a hurry' I was pulling at the bit like a young horse full of feed. The need to speed my life up to a more acceptable level had manifested itself in occasionally gunning the motor of my Morris 1100 in the streets of Kingaroy and frequenting as many dances as I could in the old country halls dotted around the South Burnett.

Still very much the wet season, I stepped out of the plane at Katherine in early March to be almost flattened by the overwhelming humidity. The manager, Tim Doran, greeted me in an old Land Rover. Besides numerous cattle stations, Vestey owned approximately fifty per cent of the shares in Land Rover as well as the Blue Star shipping line and various meat works.

In contrast to the desolation I expected, two and half metre-high spear grass and a tropical scrub land greeted me as we travelled the 11 km to the homestead that night. I was shown to my quarters where mosquitos the size of cows and black stink bugs fiercely fought the fly gauze all night to gain access to the electric light or my blood and I woke early the next morning to begin my exploration of the station's lay-out. I greatly appreciated the lush surrounds in lieu of the perceived harsh isolation somehow embedded in my imagination.

Towards the 'big house' (manager's residence) from the quarters stood a large old cottage in which the head stockman lived. The kitchen followed and turned out to be the busy centre of the entire area where all meals were prepared, including bread baking. A short path led to the girls' quarters and toilet, the area where many snakes, usually pythons, were found and caught. The dining room was located to the north of the kitchen where all staff from the manager downwards took their meals, wheeled in on a trolley from the kitchen by one of the Aboriginal domestic staff. By virtue of the large number of people that had to be fed, meal times were surprisingly orderly.

North again and joined by a covered path was the 'big house' complete with tennis court. To the east of the kitchen grew a large Tamarind tree under which a long table and chairs were placed. This provided an ideal cool spot for smoko and was a welcome relief from the steamy humidity.

More or less east from there was the meat house, a gauze wire-enclosed shed for hanging the 'killer' and salting beef. The story goes that many years before my time, an old Chinese cook went out at 4 am to get steak for breakfast. He discovered he was unable to get to the beef house door because it was being closely guarded by six metres of saltwater crocodile from the Katherine River running nearby.

Heading away to the north east from the meat house, a mango tree, Poinciana and Golden Shower trees lined the entrance to the complex via the stock yards and saddle shed. This also incorporated a killing pen surrounded by several Townsville Lucerne paddocks.

From the meat house across the entry road stood the store. This stocked anything from horseshoe nails to hobnailed boots. Every imaginable need was catered for in that shed, supervised at the time by the tireless and patient Jim Jackson, after whom the Katherine Racecourse is named. Close by could be found an extensive workshop area with the competent Warry Weggert as its resident mechanic. An old ramshackle building was located south of what was called White City for reasons no one was able to define. It stored salt and licks for cattle.

Down the river a couple of hundred metres was the 'black's camp' consisting of steel-framed corrugated iron huts with verandas out front. The entire station complex was erected on the levy bank of the Katherine River and all the buildings were quite old but, as with all Vestey properties, they were kept painted red and white and lawns and gardens were never less than immaculate. This picturesque homestead area is now a welcoming caravan park.

The Townsville Lucerne paddocks close to the homestead area gave way to Black Spring paddock, another tropical wonderland with a large spring in the middle of it. It was followed by four more Townsville Lucerne paddocks of eight hundred hectares each.

Star Dust, my very first breaker at Manbulloo station, Northern Territory.

Smoko area at Manbulloo homestead.

Manbulloo Station homestead

Six to eight km down the river from the homestead area stood an old meat works with the relics of an army camp and bomber strip, all of which extended over a few square kilometres and was utilised during World War Two.

Liger Yard was to be found further down the river on the levy bank. Bottom King yard was near the junction of the King and Katherine rivers. We used to camp safely on the banks of the rivers in those days without a thought of the saltwater crocodiles that prolifically inhabited northern waterways. They were disposed of when necessary and were consequently timid of human presence, unlike today where their protection has caused them to lose their fear of humans.

Heading out from the station down the highway, turning off to the Bomber strip and proceeding on, one went bush via MC, the first bore out from the homestead. It was at this camp that I saw my first and only min min light, a strange and unexplained phenomenon that made the hackles stand up on the back of my neck. I was attending to a call of nature shortly after tea one night and had wandered some hundred metres or more from the camp. On my return, this strange light inexplicably appeared an indefinite distance away, rising and falling in an undulating manner, advancing and retreating seemingly at will. Thinking it must have been one of the other stockmen on a similar expedition as my own, I returned to the campfire and made discreet enquiries as to which other person had required a relief trip into the bushes. All were present and vehemently denied my accusations of a prank. The light remains a mystery to this day.

Redbank was a creek crossing halfway between MC and Cowai. Before reaching Redbank, there was a small black soil plain full of devil-devil holes, as were all the small black soil plains at Manbulloo. The holes were about thirty centimetres deep scattered every metre or so apart and we dared not gallop our horses over them. It was home to a bull that had suffered a broken neck or similar in his younger days and whose head was consequently attached side-on. For a beast that could only look sideways, he was impossible to muster on horseback. I think a bull catcher later caught up with him so I imagine he made hamburger mince eventually.

Cowai had a cattle yard and holding paddock and was later the centre of several Townsville Lucerne paddocks. The yard was built surrounding a big lagoon just off the King River. Wongalla was a trap yard[35] and main centre for the back end of the run. We spent quite a lot of time here during mustering. Whip Hole was located towards Dry River from Wongalla and further up the King River on the eastern end of the run stood another trap yard, Longreach. There was also a bore and yard called Limestone at the most distant western part of the run, not far from the Willeroo boundary. At the end of the season, a couple of us would be armed with supplies and a pump and sent out to empty the small watering holes on the river. This forced cattle to drink at the main trap yards and ensured a clean muster. We had a jackaroo with us on one occasion, city-born and bred. At night the old mopoke owls would give their mournful distant call and when we assured the lad that it was the mating calls of the crocodiles in the water holes, he smartly shifted his swag to the top of the trailer.

The Katherine River formed the northern border of Manbulloo and ran the full length of the boundary. Apart from the beauty of such a water course, an outstanding

---

35 A yard with spear gates allowing cattle into the yard but not back out.

Cowai billabong, Manbulloo Station.

feature was the amount of 'feed' trees for such creatures as flying foxes. During the day, these animals lived or camped in the Katherine Gorge approximately 48 km up-stream. Late in the evening and again immediately before daylight the sky would become black for up to half an hour as the flying foxes navigated between resting and feeding.

The King River cut through the middle of Manbulloo and facilitated a number of billabongs, usually a couple of hundred metres off the main channel. Cowai was the first billabong one came to. It had a trap yard built around it, constructed well before my time I'm fairly certain by Bernie Warren. Like Wongalla and Longreach, both of which were trap yards, these billabongs were covered with beautiful

Chapter 1 Manbulloo Station

Wongalla billabong, Manbulloo.

water lilies. In the shallow edges, by torch light with a bit of meat on a string, we would catch flathead fish.

Being comprised of mostly sandy loam interspersed with small black soil plains, odd limestone ridges and watered by the Katherine and King River, Manbulloo Station was extremely poor cattle country in my opinion. Because of its impoverished quality, neither horses nor cattle thrived there. Consequently, many horses were brought in from other Vestey properties. Snip, a bay mare from Oban station and Bluey, a grey Morestone station mare were both in my string and proved exceptionally reliable when one was throwing a bull. Both would graze calmly a short but safe distance from the action and patiently wait until the beast was tied.

I must say experience is gained very quickly if one wants to enjoy a long and healthy life. Just after arriving at Manbulloo, Tim had a couple of hundred over-grown bull calves and mickeys that were too poor to deal with at the end of the previous 'dry'. Our first task was to cut and brand these cattle. I had taken the job as a first-year jackaroo[36], not knowing what skills were expected. As we were processing these animals, I grabbed and scruffed any that escaped from the worn-out calf cradle while the allegedly more experienced lads watched on. I was immediately promoted. Further experience occurred on one of the initial musters out towards MC bore. We had to throw the first mob of cattle we came across, letting them up a couple at a time to be shouldered back together until we had the nucleus of a coacher mob. I had thrown a couple of mickeys and was starting to get a bit full of myself when I jumped off to an old, moth-eaten bull with horns. I miscalculated my timing and he found his second wind. Clinging to his tail, I couldn't pull him down so round and round we went with me determinedly holding on to his green pea-soupy tail, the bull's head only inches away from my gut at every

---

36 An apprentice stockman

turn. I couldn't topple him and was too scared to let him go! There was a sapling nearby about as big as my forearm, the only chance I had to break the cycle. With steeled nerves, I dived behind it. Opposite me, the bull had a horn on either side of the sapling and was trying his best to reach me. Now what? Still stalemate and another jackaroo sat watching me from the safety of his horse all the while, not game to help. I quickly reckoned that my hat would feel less pain than me so I threw it on the ground to one side and made my exit fast while the bull continued his quarrel with my hat. One rapidly learns that judgment and timing are critically important in the bush.

My faithful mare was still waiting for me. Hazel was an Oban Station mare and when fresh, she could root fairly well. She also had a tendency to girth-gall[37] almost immediately she was cinched up. She soon became a favourite as she would fearlessly go straight in on the blade[38] of bulls or mickeys being put in with the coaches if they attempted any further escape and drive them back into the mob.

There was also a good sort of grey mare of Arab descent. Someone had apparently attempted to break her in but she was obviously sour and uncooperative and could buck pretty well too. She had been bucked in the rodeo string for two years. As I was getting a bit cocky with my recent upgrade from first year jackaroo and had ridden a few pig

---

37 Scalding caused by the girth.
38 Shoulder.

rooters, she was put in my string, possibly with the aim of 'sorting me out'. I eventually exhibited her in both led and ridden classes at the Katherine show.

Growing up, my relationship with my father was not the best. Being the third son with an only daughter following me, I believe parental focus shifted at that point. The phrase I will remember coming from my father until I die, if only for its repetitiveness, is 'You need your bloody head red.' When I look back on my childhood, I can understand that some might argue and agree with Dad. As a result, I grew up with an inferiority complex and always had to prove myself. As I matured, I did finally find a way to deal with my issues. A quote comes to mind. 'You may be disappointed if you fail, but you are doomed if you don't try.'

The way forward was revealed at Ligers yard down the Katherine River. We had four rodeo riders with us for a month, fit, active and full of pranks. One evening, I was their target. I was hanged from a tree (fortunately not unto death). Strangely, it was this incident that turned my 'introvert' into an 'extrovert' and I began taking the mickey out of myself before anyone else had the opportunity.

It was a little further down the river that Warwick Bates, nicknamed Scales for his affinity to snakes, had an altercation with a strapping four- or five-year-old bull that broke away from the mob. Scales took off after him intending to throw him. As he jumped off his horse to grasp the tail, the bull's hooves whistled past his ears and Scales

Chapter 1   Manbulloo Station

Part of the horse plant at MC Bore 1969.

landed flat on his back. He was wearing a sloppy green jumper and back at the mob 180 metres away, the bull could be seen hooking Scales' jumper, missing his stomach by what must have only been a centimetre or two. Fortunately, one of the rodeo riders who was an experienced bushman competent in all cattle handling skills galloped in and took the bull away from the fallen stockman. Poor old Scales spent the rest of the day a lighter shade of pale and didn't utter a single word. Scales had a couple of other similar

Two old gentlemen of the highest calibre. Ben on the left and Larry at Wongalla billabong 1969.

incidents along the way but this incident highlighted the point that one always went with a mate for back-up.

We had a good crew of both Aboriginal and white stockmen. Larry and Ben, two of the Aboriginal stockmen were extra-special people, both of whom could track a cockroach across concrete. A couple of Ord River colts just out from the horse breaker took off from Wongalla. Larry and Ben were horse-tailers at the time and after

Chapter 1 Manbulloo Station

getting our dinner camp horses ready, Ben left to locate the escapees. He was gone for two days taking neither food or spare horses and came back with the runaways without fuss. These two men, along with Manbulloo Pat and Blucher were clever stockmen and great blokes.

While at Manbulloo, I learned one of the most valuable of life's lessons about the right and wrong way of doing things. I discovered I learned more from seeing how difficult it was doing things the wrong way. While Tim Doran ran an efficient and well-organised ship, the next manager tried too many short-cuts and back-to-front ways of doing things. His methods usually prolonged the job or meant doing it all over again.

Jim Jackson was the bookkeeper/store keeper. One day, Larry's wife Nida came to the store for a 'milk trousher'. Understandably, Jim didn't understand and asked Nida again what she wanted, getting the same response: 'Milk trousher.' Eventually, cupping her hands under her pendulous mammaries, she convinced Jim that she wanted a bra.

On Friday evenings I was usually asked to take the truck filled with the station's Aboriginal families to the pictures. We young whites would go on Saturday evenings. At interval, most of the lads would go across the road to Kirby's pub, but Scales and I, pure and innocent as we were, went to March Motors instead (now a Camping and Fishing shop) furnished with our own spoons and consumed five family bricks of ice cream (the equivalent of five litres). After the pictures, I ran the 11 km home and woke the next morning fresh and ready to go while the others still nursed their sore heads.

Camp cooks were temperamental and touchy 'creatures' to say the least. One young Manbulloo jackaroo made a habit of sitting on a camp oven beside the fire each night so one evening, old Dave shovelled a generous heap of live coals into the camp oven and placed it in the unsuspecting culprit's favourite spot. I'm sure if an inspection of bare bums had taken place, the lad's buttocks would have borne the rosy imprint of a camp oven.

Apart from their volatile and prickly dispositions, camp cooks came armed with their own camp tucker menus. With Dave, corned beef with damper was a staple. Then there was Burdekin Duck and Mysteries in their overcoats. Burdekin Duck was comprised of slices of corn beef in batter, and Mysteries were made of... chunks of corned beef in batter! We could hardly complain about a lack of variety.

The Stockcamp Cook (with a lot of 'poetic license')

You've heard about the drover's cook
Who had one bloodshot eye?
No laces in his ragged boots
Or buttons on his fly.

Chapter 1 Manbulloo Station

You've heard about his hairy paws
And pants hitched up with wire
But what about the stock camp cook
Setting stockmen's pants on fire?

A cook's pots are his pride and joy
Like an old hen with her brood,
No one else dares use those pans
For fear of being sued.

Now one young lout had eyed the pans
A rather brash young fool.
And then one day he grabbed a pot
To use it for a stool.

The camp cook lowered his shaggy head
And swore beneath his breath
Then eloquently he warned the boy
To save himself from death.

Now some folks don't learn lessons fast
And some are just plain dumb.
The boy still sought the biggest pot
On which to park his bum.

But then one day, the Cook's worm turned
And Cookie grasped the pot
He filled it full of fiery coals
'Til it glowered red and hot.

The pot had lost its fiery flush
When the stockmen shuffled in.
The old cook dropped his head again
To hide a wicked grin.

The lad heaped food upon his plate
And filled his mug with tea.
Then settled on the biggest pot,
With plate upon his knee.

It seemed the world stood still that night
And silence reigned supreme.
Until the air was torn to shreds
With agonising screams!

Plate and mug winged through the dark
The boy soared to his feet.
He danced in time to his mournful howl
And slapped his glowering seat.

He plunged into the cattle trough
To put the fire out.
No one looked and no one laughed
At the poor, unwary lout.

And what about the cook you ask?
Well, he dropped his shaggy head.
But his belly shook with soundless mirth
'Til finally he said:

'I hope that that'll learn ya mate,
You don't mess with me gear.
I've warned a hundred times before
'n I thought I'd made it clear.

But nah, you wouldn't listen mate,
From ear to ear you're bone
So let me say it one more time …
Leave me bloody pots alone!'

©Val Wicks

Tim Doran came mustering down by the old army reserve where there were concrete slabs, remnant of the war time army barracks. Head stockman Des Stenhouse, Tim and I were doing a sweep out from the coaches on one particularly cloudy day when we rode past an old Crown stove sitting on one of these slabs. Des and Tim were yapping away when fifteen minutes later, we rode past the same Crown stove again. We'd done a full circle. Cloudy weather and chin-wagging had led to acute embarrassment in front of the new kid on the block! On another occasion, we were bending the lead of a mob of about eight head in long spear grass when they all bafflingly vanished. Retracing our tracks and venturing about 10 m towards where the lead had gone, we discovered the mob had dropped to their bellies as one and were lying flat in the long grass, motionless.

It was here at Manbulloo that I learned the unique method Aboriginal people employed to depict how close or far an object or place might be. We were returning from attending a muster with Gilbert Pollock on Dry River Station and it seemed as if we would *never* get back to Whip Hole where we were camped. I rode around to the lead where Larry was.

'How far, old man?' I asked him. Jutting his lips out in the direction we were travelling, he replied. 'Little bit long way.' My curiosity was satisfied. Had we been droving bullocks down the Canning Stock Route, his response would have been 'Properly long way.'

When I had my collarbone dislocated by a horse rolling over the top of me, 'light duties' came in the form of driving the old Bedford truck picking up bulls the camp had thrown and tied to trees. On the way to the meat works fully loaded, thankfully with Des on board, I breasted the top of a ridge after turning on to the bitumen. On the down-hill side 180 metres away stood a policeman, right in the middle of the road. He was allegedly doing vehicle checks and indicated with hand signals for me to stop. I applied the brakes in compliance but nothing happened even though I had started to change down a gear or two. We had apparently torn a brake line off while driving through the bush to pick up the bulls. The closer I got to the policeman, the more agitated became his hand gestures until he finally extricated himself

Des Stenhouse, a better head stockman never found. Riding Twitter at Wongalla 1969.

from the bullbar with Des yelling 'No brakes!' I was terror-stricken, wondering how long I would be staying in Fanny Bay goal! With Des's explaining to a recomposed officer of the law, I was requested to present at the police station on Monday with my driver's license and brakes in good order.

I learned to empathise with the drovers who used to drove mobs of 1,200 bullocks across the Murrinji and the difficulties they experienced. One night, we had to 'night watch' the cattle in a broken-down wire yard at Top King as we mustered towards Cowai. The evening before, a cow we mustered had a calf planted somewhere in the grass. I went on watch at midnight and not long into the watch, a dingo discovered and mauled the calf. Its bellowing brought the entire mob to their feet in one surging rush. When one experiences around 200 head of sleeping cattle jump and run blindly as I did that night, every hair stands on end and the heart feels close to exploding out of the chest! Thankfully, the cattle only went across the yard about sixty metres or so before pulling up.

Another episode that cranked my heart rate sky high occurred at the station while we were shoeing and riding our fresh plant horses. I was allocated a bay ex-Ord River mare broken in the previous year. When I rode her in the station yards, she rooted but was easily rideable so I asked to be let out into the Townsville Lucerne paddock where the roadway entered into the station precinct. As I eased the mare into a trot, she abruptly grabbed the bit and bolted.

Chapter 1 Manbulloo Station

Now a lot of people have ridden a horse that 'takes off' but that is completely different to a 'bolter'. No matter how hard I tried, I couldn't bend the mare so I tried to make her buck by thumbing her up the shoulder. I had no luck there either. She was galloping flat out, seemingly blind to her surrounds and all but took the gate with all fours sliding out from under her. I was determined to stay on board as she regained her feet, thinking I might now have control but she took flight again, this time towards the fence at the river where we again ended leg up! The conclusion of this event came some weeks later when she and I were mustering out bush. We galloped to bend a cow that had broken from the mob and as we went in to shoulder her back, the cow propped, threw her head at the horse's flank and disembowelled her on the spot.

CHAPTER 2

Off to Spring Creek Station

Tim and Joc returned from a brief stint down south and were transferred to Spring Creek Station about 113 km from Kununurra. Spring Creek was a relatively small station but very rough. Bower birds, conkerberry bushes and spring-fed creeks were features, along with towering rocky hills and rugged country. If one wasn't riding up steep inclines, one was sliding down.

Rod and I transferred across to Spring Creek at Tim's request. It had no airstrip and only 32 volt power. Once again, we had great Aboriginal staff, namely Joe Kelly, Albert, Limbunya Jimmie and Teddy.

Spring Creek horses were generally of smaller stature but as hard as the rocks they were born on. We always carried a saddle bag with at least two spare shoes, hammer

Chapter 2   Off to Spring Creek Station

Sophie and Andrew, nicknamed Minnie, with Albert, Jimmy, Joe and Teddy at Spring Creek Station 1971.

and nails and after nearly every run we would need to replace a couple of shoes. One day, on a chestnut horse named Bob, I was at full speed turning a lead when we hit a slab of limestone about three metres across. It was like concrete and my knee was almost touching the slab when Bob regained his footing and we reached the other side. The smell of smoking hooves and horseshoe being torn off still lingers in my nostrils!

Tim was no rough rider but he always encouraged us

louts to have a go. As a result, we often put a 'kicker' on a station horse if it showed an inclination to buck. It was here that I learned I was not a bull rider but I enjoyed moderate success in saddle bronc and bareback events.

We 'packed'[39] up the Bells Creek to muster. In a packhorse camp, one has the barest essentials: a swag as thick as a cigarette, an axe, a pea rifle, flour, tea and sugar. On reaching camp, one would kill a beast to supply the meat. When we arrived at our destination, part of the fence was demolished and rolled up like a ball of steel wool. Strutting about in the paddock were two large bull camels. As Tim handed me the .22 rifle, his orders were plain.

'No live camels to be left in the paddock.' Up to that point, I had never seen a camel before, much less understood how they operated. As I marched towards my quarry, I carefully observed the stunted height of the predominant Snappy Gum trees. Likewise, the camels carefully observed the stunted stature of the game hunter. They quickly circled and headed straight for me. Did I say something earlier about a heart condition? Thankfully, they halted some 140 metres short to better observe the intruder, at which point I realised I was looking almost directly up their nostrils! Not a promising target for a poor marksman with heart palpitations! Several shots later, the unsavoury task was completed. Later on, when I was sent to manage both Spring and Mistake Creek, we had a mob of about seventy

---

39 Used pack horses

Chapter 2 Off to Spring Creek Station

camels who sometimes became a nuisance when we were mustering with helicopters. Otherwise, once they knew where the fences were, they seldom did any damage.

Another station joined Spring Creek on the northern side but was cut off from its main portion and homestead by the Ord River. As a result, they never mustered their country on our side of the river. On two occasions they sent us messages to say they were coming over to muster and we needed to attend. Old Albert and I were sent and on our arrival at the designated spot with packhorses in tow, no one turned up. It drizzled rain that night and I wound up with our rations in my swag with me to keep them dry. Someone had to care for the unattended cattle so Albert and I mustered all the way back to our yards.

As fate would have it, I ended up managing both Spring Creek and Mistake Creek Stations some years later. By this time, the aforementioned station was mustering their country across the Ord. As responsible managers do, one informs the neighbours of one's intent to do a boundary muster and invites them to attend as it was all open-range country without fenced boundaries. After duly sending memos and telegrams to our northern neighbour, no response was received so we proceeded to helicopter muster where I reckoned our mutual boundary to be. On completion of the muster, I noticed a Toyota parked on the Duncan Road. It didn't take a genius to work out who it was so with hand gesticulations from the chopper, I invited the occupant back home to wait while the cattle were brought in. As one can imagine, it's not possible to discern earmarks or brands on galloping cattle from thirty metres in the air. However, dismounting from the chopper and greeting my unannounced visitor he left me in no doubt about my pedigree — illegitimate and a 'cattle duffer[40]'! Strangely enough, I kept my cool and invited him in for a coffee while we waited for the 400 head to arrive. During that time, I caught my camp horse and assured the man that all 'strangers' in the mob would be cut out, thus guaranteeing no calves would be wrongly branded.

"If we have been mustering your country, there should be quite a number of "strangers", I told him as I rode away to perform the draft. We cut out seven cows and calves and I informed him there were only four or five dry cows and several steers. Whilst my deflated guest said he believed me, he took up my proposal to take my horse and check for himself before driving away with a hopefully different point of view about my 'pedigree'. There were some other issues including these neighbours but I believe they reflect too poorly on the cattle industry and are best left un-recalled.

At a later date while helicopter mustering with Eric Webb, an experienced stockman and chopper pilot, we were having difficulty putting a couple of mickeys into the mob. Flying at tree-top level and while Eric was concentrating on his view, I was hanging off the skid. I dropped to the

---

40   Cattle thief.

Chapter 2 Off to Spring Creek Station

ground and threw the mickey. Eric landed the helicopter immediately after and rebuked me thoroughly for my lack of understanding about balancing aircraft and aerodynamics in general.

'Just tell me if you're going to do that next time,' he scolded.

Joe Kelly, one of the Aboriginal stockmen, came up from the camp to tell the manager's wife Joc that his wife Nora wouldn't talk to him. Nora had been an excellent kitchen off-sider for a long time until she had broken her ankle in her later years. From then on, she was basically bed-ridden and advancing old age was also becoming a factor.

It was revealed that Nora's refusal to talk to Joe meant that she had slipped into a coma and was desperately ill. The Flying Doctor was called up and we needed to get the old lady to the Rosewood station air strip some 50 km away.

Our best means of transport for a coma patient was in the back of Tim's Valiant station wagon with the back seat down. Off to the camp we went to pick up the patient. The corrugated iron room was dimly lit and smelt like a urinal. The unfortunate patient was gargling on copious amounts of chewing-tobacco-stained mucus and saliva, the sound of which still haunts me today! With Tim and Joc each grasping Nora under the armpits, I was happy to take hold of her feet, furthest away from the awful sounds she was making. What I had not expected was the state of the lower legs and ankles. I hadn't realised that the only toilet facility she was capable of using was probably the side of the cyclone stretcher on which she slept. When we placed her on the mattress in the back of the car, I feared I would have to surgically remove my sweaty grip from her legs. (Each time I think about it, I still want to wash my hands thoroughly!)

Even with a front window seat, the journey to the airstrip was difficult as the smell associated with the gargling and the vivid remembrance of the feet were busily disturbing my delicate and un-initiated psyche. As if it was remotely possible, the worst was yet to come!

We waited for approximately fifteen minutes for the plane to arrive during which time I couldn't bring myself to be within hearing range of the awful gasping gurgles. When the doctor arrived, duty called and we transferred the patient from the mattress onto the RFDS stretcher. Before taking to the air again, Nora's airways had to be unblocked. The doctor inserted a clear plastic tube down Nora's throat, then placing his mouth over the end of the tube, he proceeded to suck up the vilest-looking fluid to within a couple of centimetres from his lips. Placing his finger over the top, he emptied the fluid onto the ground. At that precise point, the contents of my stomach began desperately knocking on the door to be let out. I quickly retreated a safe distance until the doctor was satisfied and my stomach had settled down. The sucking process was continued until all the offending phlegm and mucus had been removed and if I ever doubt the dedication of medical people, my mind harks back to this incident.

Chapter 2 Off to Spring Creek Station

Nora returned home from hospital a few months later but passed away not long after that. It is always a sad time when a station hand dies, regardless of race or creed because they are 'family' and fulfill an essential role in station life.

Vestey used to put on an annual race meeting come rodeo which was originally held close to where the Negri River joins the Ord River, hence the name Negri Picnic Rraces and Rodeo. Due to resumption of that area for regeneration for the Ord River Dam, the meeting was moved to the Linacre Creek on Ord River Station. Because of further resumptions, it was moved again to No. 23 bore on Nicholson Station. It was from Spring Creek that Albert and I walked our race and sports horses the 177 km for the meeting, camping halfway at the old Ord River homestead on the banks of the Forrest River.

During my time at Spring Creek, we helped the Mistake Creek stock camp to do one of the first helicopter musters. A suitable site was selected on the Stirling River, portable yards set up and long wings camouflaged with Bloodwood branches run out in preparation for the muster. Stewart Skogland was the pilot and the muster was a great success with many old piker bullocks and clean skin bulls in the yard.

Spring Creek and Mistake Creek were both amazing places to work with so many beautiful creeks and rivers weaving among rocky hills and included the northern end of the Osmond Range where the Bungle Bungles are situated.

It was after only one season at Spring Creek that two

events loomed on the horizon. My number came up in the draft for the Vietnam War and I was instructed to have a 'medical'. I was as fit as the proverbial Malley bull but in spite of Tim and Doctor McConnel's adamant denials, I was sure they must have conspired to get me out of what turned into an unjust war and left those who were involved more mentally than physically traumatised. I was declared 'unfit' for service!

The other option was a job as head stockman at Nicholson Station, about 180 km further south towards Halls Creek.

One of the first helicopter musters on the Stirling river — Stewie Skogland was the pilot.

CHAPTER 3

Nicholson's 'Head Boy'

Len and Robyn Hill were managing Nicholson when I arrived there to take up the head stockman position. Len was one of the last drovers to go down the Canning Stock Route. His book *Droving with Ben Taylor* is an historical 'must read'. Nicholson was mostly fairly open downs country but did have some rough spots as well. Lighthouse, Bamboo and of course Morella Gorge, the gorge now being on the maps as a place of beauty and interest.

At this time, Nicholson camp comprised of all Aboriginal labour with Len directing operations aerial mustering into portable yards at Brook Creek on the far northern end of the property. I was dropped off at this site and spent the morning in the bull dust before going on to Nicholson for lunch. Nicholson was a central location for the service of several stations and therefore had a lot of staff. Indeed,

Len Hill, Canning stock route drover and wife Robyn, ex hospital matron, 'chef' and none better to be found.

it was akin to a small township. Mrs Hill ran the dining room along old Victorian principles. Everything was in scrupulous order with starched white tablecloths, highly polished serviette rings and staff 'waiting' on the table. Covered in red bull dust, I was directed to the men's ablution block where I did my best to clean up for lunch. Bear in mind that I didn't yet know the bookkeeper or most of the staff. I arrived at my allocated position on the manager's immediate right, alongside the middle-aged and

Chapter 3 Nicholson's 'Head Boy'

'proper' female bookkeeper. I seem to remember her name was Norma. Far from just saying 'Hello, pleased to meet you,' Norma peered at me intently for a second.

'My, you have dirty ears,' she said. Welcome to your new home.

Horse mustering was due to commence as the wet was clearing, horses to be drafted, breaking-in to do and a plant to get ready for the upcoming season. The locals were off driving very unreliable vehicles at this point and if you ever watched the TV documentary *Bush Mechanics*, you will understand the calibre of vehicle that rolled in and out of the station camp. Approximately 180 km away, Halls Creek was their weekend venue to visit relatives and to enjoy the disastrous effects of the new-found 'demon drink'. I had told them of the intention to muster the horses on Monday and that they should all be ready to carry out this task.

Monday morning arrived and Riley had the horses in the yard ready to go but no Cuddy who was the self-proclaimed 'head boy'. One other was missing too, probably Albert. I instructed that their horses should be left in the yard so they could catch up. After all, they knew the country better than I did. A couple of hundred metres into our mission, the two absentees arrived high-stepping and still as drunk as lords. On observing their totally unfit state to even stay on a horse, much less go mustering, I 'politely' but firmly informed them their services wouldn't be required any longer. Cuddy's jovial and alcohol-infused demeanour switched off like a light and he became belligerent.

'You can't work 'im for dis bloke! You fella all gotta pullout,' he roared at his mates. In the blink of an eye the rest of the team had the saddles pulled off their horses and were gone back to the camp. This left just David and me so we continued on a leisurely ride down the Nicholson River.

As it was the end of the 'wet', income and rations were meagre and most stock camp workers were happy to get back on to station tucker and have an income again. I might add I had been told these people could be difficult to work. However, things happen for a reason (experience for one) and the next day found a procession of men coming to the saddle shed.

'Malluka, any shance of a shob?' I put them off, telling them to come back on Monday morning, and they came — probably twenty-five men assembled, ready to begin. I selected the ones I wanted, dismissing the rest and I had the best team I could ever have hoped for. These men would walk through fire to help and I was now 'Head Boy.'

It was my opinion that the previous head stockman should not have been allowed near the horse yard. Pretty much every one of the previous year's breakers were not working horses but rather 'saddle broncs'. Len had bred an incredibly fine line of station thoroughbreds, sixteen hands with a ton of guts and intelligence. However, if you didn't work them, they would certainly give you a working-over.

Chapter 3 Nicholson's 'Head Boy'

Once pulled into gear, a better horse was hard to find and some were sold back to England as 'eventing' horses.

My first foray into racing was unimpressive to say the least. Knowing nothing about the Sport of Kings, I simply ran several old stagers with only moderate success. One spoilt youngster broken in the previous year was a horse called Sultan. He almost threw me several times in quick succession one morning but with a bit of persuasion using the buckle end of a bull strap when he bucked, we finally reached an amicable agreement. Sultan went on to become a place-getter as a ladies' horse in the Negri Races Ladies race.

Another of these horses was one that was always allocated to Sugarday, one of the Aboriginal stockmen. Sugarday was never game to open the horse up but I liked the look of the horse and offered to swap Sugarday for one of mine. Woodsman could buck and strike at the bit with the best of them and was a difficult customer to deal with. I nominated him in the 'Maiden race' over 800 m and bought him in the Calcutta for a lousy ten dollars, the rank outsider. On the morning before the race, he took off rooting and striking at the bit and I doubted I would find anyone who would be anxious to ride him.

Race morning dawned and Woodsman was to run in the first race at 12.30 pm. In the saddling paddock he gazed about almost as if he was saying 'Boy, a lot of people have come out to see me.' He trotted out on to the track, behaved himself and won the race by several lengths. Almost while he was still running, I realised I hadn't nominated him to race on the second day. Rushing to the secretary's office, I designated him for the President's Handicap over 1,400 metres just two races away.

Woodsman missed the jump out of the barriers in this second race by about four lengths. By the time he reached the first bend at the back straight he had caught up and cantered on home to win by five lengths.

Of the eleven horses I had starting over that weekend, Nicholson horses won eight races. Our poorest performance was a fourth place in the Oaks Maiden for fillies. Shiloh won that race while Carissma came fourth. Tiger Tim won the Hunters Plate over jumps and although we didn't place in the camp draft on Gamble, a horse educated by Neil Dudgeon, we did well. Without question, Nicholson horses were the most versatile and capable horses I ever threw a leg across.

While at Nicholson, we also competed at the Halls Creek Races and Rodeo with the Underwoods, Quilties and of course the Moola Bulla crew. Tommy Quilty was always a fierce competitor and relegated me to second fiddle in all three rough stock events. I came good in the foot race though, having been purchased by big John Underwood for $110 in the Calcutta. I honoured his faith in my ability by narrowly beating the well-favoured Gilbo MacAdam. What a great bloke Gilbo is!

As with all Vestey stations, Nicholson's Aboriginal

Chapter 3   Nicholson's 'Head Boy'

pensioners received weekly rations of essentials. As these provisions only came to the station as 'wet' season and 'dry' season orders, they comprised a loaded road train that had to be dealt with. Dalgety Dick, so called for his previous employment with Dalgety, was the storekeeper. He had previously given out a new version of Greenlight wax matches and had demonstrated their use to an old pensioner named Tomato by lighting them after dipping them in a billy can of water, proving that even in wet conditions, they would light. On his return the following week, Dick asked Tomato if he wanted more of those matches.

'Nah. Too many hum-bug carrying dat billy can of water round all 'a time,' Tomato replied.

Bunda came up to me one day as serious as the Pope.

'Malluka, I bin t'ink it in my brain ...' I was pleased that was where he was thinking and smiled for the rest of the day! I always found those in my employ easy to humour and they gave me great occasions for a good laugh many times.

It was at Nicholson that my interest in the fairer form of humanity peaked. A certain blond Rhodesian apparently travelling to look for better genetics arrived as the new domestic. In spite of a brief but rough start, she managed to get under my guard and we soon became engaged.

One must keep a straight face on certain occasions but I had great difficulty one day when I was called on to administer some medical assistance. Flying Doctor kits on stations are filled with medicines, all of which were numbered so that, after symptoms were described over the air to the doctor in Wyndham, he would instruct which number was to be used or administered.

I was relief manager at Nicholson and was newly engaged to Val, the Rhodesian. She needed an injection of five cc of Number 74, a penicillin suspension for an infection she had. The aged bookkeeper (or so she seemed to a twenty-two-year-old male) needed a dose of Number 86, also to be administered into the muscle. I proceeded to draw down the appropriate medication and headed off to the women's quarters where the two patients were eagerly awaiting the handsome young 'doctor'! I asked who wanted to be first and my fiancé volunteered, rolling up her sleeve. I swabbed the top of her very appealing arm and pushed the needle in. A fair bit of inoculating cattle with five-in-one and three-day sickness vaccines helps develop a certain finesse with needle and syringe!

My bedside manner changed when the bookkeeper asked me to wait 'just a moment' as she disappeared into her room. Shortly after, she called out 'Righto' from behind her closed door. Entering in with my loaded syringe, it's difficult to describe my feelings as I approached the now bed-ridden patient with her ivory white buttocks protruding into the open air from under the sheets. Choking back the bubble of laughter that threatened to erupt and make this task more difficult to execute, I visually quartered the right bum cheek and drove the needle home. She was

Three of the best L to R — Davey Dempster, Val and Neil Hogg 1973.

much obliged and thankfully didn't require any further treatment.

Shortly thereafter, we were appointed caretakers of Flora Valley Station over the wet season in 1973. There had allegedly been some shady cattle dealing going on, thus making the management position vacant.

On the way home to Flora from a Hall's Creek town trip, we stopped to pick up a person walking along the road a long way from anywhere. His name was Bobby and it wasn't much later that we received a radio message enquiring as to whether we had seen a certain individual who sounded suspiciously like our hitchhiker. If we did, could we please let the authorities know? We told them about our passenger and the following morning, Sean Murphy, delegated (honorary) constabulary arrived at Flora with handcuffs. Bobby was headed back to complete his stint in gaol. It turned out that he was a low-risk miscreant and a police officer had told him on the day of his escape, 'The sooner I see the back of you, the happier I'll be.' No doubt it was the officer's job to cook and care for his inmates and one less to feed, the better. Bobby took him at his word and 'helped him out' by taking off when his back was turned.

Bobby heading back to finish his prison stint

CHAPTER 4

A stint at Helen Springs

After four months at Flora when a very wet 'wet' was drawing to a close, Val and I were sent to Helen Springs Station where I was to run the stock camp.

We were married there at 2 pm on 16 April 1974. I'm not sure if Val had ulterior motives as she'd organised a Reverend Plaice to officiate (something 'fishy' was about to take place!). That was forty-eight years ago and I still have the hook in my mouth!

During our time on Flora Valley, a Christian woman named Carol and Val engaged in some lengthy discussions about God. As a result, we were both baptised for the forgiveness of our sins, which were *many*, on Helen Springs. When one stops to consider how three Christian men from the heart of Sydney managed to find us at No. 8 bore over and along approximately 90-100 km of station roads and fence lines seeking Val, one must surely believe in the providence of God!

A common misconception about Christians is that they are portrayed thinking they are better and more 'righteous' than their fellow man. The truth is that fair-dinkum Christians admit they have *serious* issues and are prepared to own their faults and try to do better, all thanks to the sacrifice Jesus made. Along with King David in Psalm 51:10 who said, 'Create in me a clean heart, oh God and renew a right spirit within me,' true Christians frequently petition God for the same grace.

Unlike the breeder country in the west, Helen Springs is located on the Barkley Tableland and comprises almost all downs country. It was primarily a bullock depot and at that time turned off thousands of fat cattle annually. Not one bullock was ever drafted in a yard. All drafting took place on horseback in open country. I always had two or three horses tied up and all they were ever asked to do was to cut out cattle.

The downs were a whole different concept to the coacher mustering of cows and calves. Camped at No. 6 bore, we were mustering fats one morning when we came upon a mob of bullocks on a bluebush swamp about 800 metres from the camp. A couple of us cantered around the lead and within fifteen minutes had around 800 bullocks blocked up, bullocks so fat one could roll a swag out on their backs.

Chapter 4 A stint at Helen Springs

Some of these would have been Limbunya 'stags', only castrated at two and a half or three years of age and as wild as hawks. After a couple of years on prime Flinders grass they were, (to quote an old mate) 'as quiet and fat as an old blue dog under a shady tree on a hot summer's day.' The 'wet' that was brought on by Cyclone Tracey flushed mobs of old bullocks out of the blue bush swamps, some shelly old gentlemen being up to twenty years old.

As a result of the good wet season and plenty of grass, there was an abundance of rodents, which meant plenty of reptiles and I would need to write another book just to tell snake stories but one stands out above the rest.

When we arrived at No. 8 trucking yard, our first job was to pump out the dip and clean it. Floating in the filthy old chemical mixture was two and a half metres of King Brown as thick as a man's arm. Blue had hind shoes to go on his little black mare so while he was away getting the horses up to catch her, the rest of us laid the dead serpent out in the stubby grass with its head in amongst his shoeing gear. When he brought his mare in, I quickly grasped her hind foot and asked Blue to pass me the rasp, which he unflinchingly did. The on-lookers gave a slight chuckle and Blue thought he must have had a hole in his jeans. Second request for shoeing implement, same result! On my third request for hammer and nails, I casually said 'Watch out for the snake.' Blue reacted as if he'd been bitten and went to work on two and half metres of King Brown with a shoeing hammer. He had picked up several bits of shoeing equipment lying a mere twenty to 30 cm from its head and hadn't seen it.

Strange things happen in unusual places, one being the Ettamogah-pub- style two-storey house at No. 8 bore alleged to be haunted. Because of this, the lads refused to camp near it. The 'haunted' label came from a combination of events. At an undetermined time in the night, just enough breeze would rise up to cause the massive wheel of the mill to turn, emitting a sort of squealing groan. This would be enough to wake a person, only for them to hear the old kerosene fridge humming downstairs. Groggy with sleep and ears full of groans and hums, it was all that was needed to upset the irrational minds of fragile youths. 'To him who is in fear, everything rustles.' (Sophocles 496 BC)

The far northern block of Helen Springs named Monmona had a hut and an old fellow caretaking there by himself. That would be enough for most and as a result 'The Monmona Madman' so resided. Helen's manager, a compassionate man took a lad out to stay and keep George company over the wet season. It's reported that on the manager's departure, the grizzled old bushman disappeared into his hut and returned with a .22 rifle. An unfortunate mudlark was sitting on a fence post just ten paces away. The old fellow drew a steady bead and shot the luckless bird in front of the lad, put the rifle down and calmly said, 'Don't try to run away.' The next time the manager came out, the

Chapter 4 A stint at Helen Springs

boy had his gear loaded on the back of the Toyota before it had even stopped.

Tim would employ anyone and on one occasion, he sent two Pommie lasses out to us. They were due to return to England in a couple of months' time and heard stories about the inexplicable min min lights. They desperately hoped to see one before they went home. We were camped at No. 5 bore somewhere between 5 and 9 km off the Barkly Stock Route. This was unknown to the girls from England. We were on the up-wind side of the route this one particular night so there was no dust or noise from the road.

We were just finishing tea when suddenly, a light appeared some kilometres back towards Elliot. As it progressed towards Eva Downs, it disappeared and re-appeared at intervals, depending on the undulation of the country. The *perfect* min min light! The girls' wish was granted. A road train soundlessly passed by and the 'min min' light that wasn't finally vanished.

CHAPTER 5

Turbulent times

It was a turbulent time for everyone when the prices of cattle slumped and we had to move a number of times including back to Manbulloo, a stint at Nutwood Station, back to Spring Creek and the Wave Hill Horse sale where Val and I were to cater for the crowd attending. This was a notable occasion as we were given the services of a professional chef who, I have to say, was a 'little different'. Jimmy was a great bloke and taught me a thing or two about catering, such as breaking eggs two at a time and how not to get flustered when mobbed by a hungry crowd.

After this rather disruptive period, we found ourselves back managing Spring Creek and Mistake Creek combined. The country was somewhat out of hand and the company wasn't prepared to spend much money, with a view to eventually selling it some years later. As a result, my

Chapter 5   Turbulent times

improvements cost them little more than chainsaw fuel, some Number 8 wire and wages. We built a timber yard at Horse Creek with a holding paddock about 5 km around. We reinforced some suspension fence holding paddocks and constructed proper timber gateways. At Bamboo in one muster, we put together about 500 head into coaches with the chopper of which about 75 per cent were unbranded. Out of several chopper musters of four to five hundred head at Horse Creek, usually 99 per cent were cleanskins, yet even then the company refused to give us a decent truck. I never was the Pastoral Inspector's golden-haired boy.

After every muster, we would cut the undesirables out and spay them so the following year we could turn off fat cows instead of having them dead in a bog-hole. The bullock paddock was notorious for spoilt cattle and with a heavy infestation of prickly acacia, the job was made that much harder. I was with Bob Coombes in the chopper spotting and when we came close to the coaches, I was to jump out and help the crew on the ground. I had just left the aircraft when I noticed that Bob had climbed to about forty-five metres and all was not well. Suddenly, the chopper plummeted to the ground. A bearing in the tail rotor had failed, leaving the chopper to auto-rotate helplessly, plunging into the paddock below. Thankfully, Bob walked away uninjured but the machine was a total write-off. I worked with many skilled pilots of which Peter Underhill and Eric Webb were exceptional and Ian Petherick had no equal.

Four main water courses ran through Mistake Creek; RB Creek on the Spring Creek side, Mistake Creek, the Negri and the Stirling. After the wet when the rivers ran clear again and before the mustering season started, we would go down to the causeway where the Duncan Road crosses the Negri and in fifteen minutes we could catch all the fish we needed for a feed. Those black bream were the best eating fish.

One of the finest horses I ever rode was a big chestnut named Imp LOT 337. He was broken in at the end of the year before I got to Mistake so was a fresh horse in my plant at the beginning of the season. I saddled him up and had ridden approximately 5 km without any fuss when right out of left field, he dropped me like a hot spud. He trotted away a few paces before turning to look at me as if to say 'Now just remember who you are dealing with.' I hopped back on and for the rest of his life with me, he never so much as tightened the girth. Over the next few years, he won both camp drafting and barrel races and was the sort of horse who only had to be shown what to do once.

The new Mistake Creek manager didn't have the same experience. Imp would throw whoever tried to ride him before condescending to let them remain on board. Some eighteen months later I was asked if I wanted to borrow him and I could barely rustle up a horse float fast enough!

On my arrival at Mistake Creek, Imp was in the stables a few metres from the kitchen/dining room. Tom suggested

Chapter 5   Turbulent times

Only ever one such horse in a life time.
Imp and Wicksie at Bull Catching camp 1980.

we have a drink of tea first. On hearing my voice, the horse looked up towards the kitchen and did not take his eyes off the door through which I had disappeared.

Having never ridden the horse bareback or with just a halter, it was my intention to do so and all the station staff lined the rails to watch me thrown on my ear. They were to be sorely disappointed. With me on his back and just a halter, this intelligent animal carried me up onto the horse float without a flinch. Later on, back in south east Queensland, Imp taught our children how to ride. He lived a few years past his thirtieth birthday and his grave and headstone are in the back yard of our home at Tingoora.

In quite a different category, several other Mistake Creek horses became famous on posters promoting travel to the Kimberly area. An amateur photographer took photos of these extreme bucking horses that later went on to adorn Ansett Airways travel posters. They gained a reputation of being some of the best in the west.

Again, we had an amazing Aboriginal workforce until an unfortunate bureaucratic decision took them away from their country. As a result, they lost their culture, dignity and the places where they were born and worked, free to go on 'walkabout' during the wet, happy to return. They were a loyal and wonderful people and I miss my old mates and fellow-workers. If they could read this, I would tell them 'I'll always remember your great service. You have left me with a lot of very good memories!'

Due to lack of support from the company and the offer of a bull-catching contract on Turner River Station, we dejectedly left a job and a place we loved for new horizons and a great 'unknown'.

Chapter 5   Turbulent times

Andy Martin on Plain Jane 1978
Des Stenhouse judging on far right.

My last buckjump ride on Lodi.
The top rail is a far better option these days.

CHAPTER 6

Love-a-bull Catchers

We built a bull-catching plant, purchased a caravan and headed into something foreign to me. Horses and cattle, hair and four legs were all I was really interested in and knew intimately. Machinery? Absolutely not! At least, that was how it started. However, it didn't take very long before the catcher became another member of myself and the nightmares disappeared. The change of mindset arrived with the commencement of building the 'catcher' and making a cattle crate for the four-wheel drive Bedford truck. An experienced bull catcher working on Mistake Creek gave me a pattern to follow. Most essentially, the five-millimetre steel belly plate, roll cage and lengthened spring hangers provided a better ride and bald tyres enabled improved manoeuvrability.

Our caravan and camp were set up next to a magnificent

Chapter 6 Love-a-bull Catchers

water hole on the Turner River a short walk from the old homestead where old Mick Coombs, a retired drover, resided.

Turner was a dream place to catch bulls providing one avoided the numerous breakaways. Immediately through the gap in the Hardman Range where the road passed through, there was a piece of ground the size of a football field surrounded by treacherous breakaways. Often there would be at least three bulls grazing on this patch and one had to work out very quickly which bull was the oldest and potentially the 'boss' of the mob. Catch a younger bull first and the rest would disappear down in the breakaways. Catch the old 'boss' first and the young ones tended to stand around gawking just long enough for me to put them down too. A bull I was chasing and which was running a metre or so in front of me on the passenger side suddenly dived off to the side as we careered down the slope. Taking a quick glimpse to see what had caused his fright, I discovered my passenger-side tyres were just centimetres from going down a two metre deep by two-and-a-half-metre wide breakaway obscured by long grass. I caught that bull another day!

It is easy to doubt the incredible strength of a bull unless one works with them. On one occasion, I was running a bull to keep him off the black soil, shouldering him with the catcher. With every galloping stride for the next 50 m, he lifted the catcher half a metre further down the ridge. Another bull I had already caught and whose front legs were tied was ready to be loaded. I approached him head-on to knock him over but forgot to engage four-wheel drive. Even in his limited capacity, he effortlessly lifted the front end of the catcher and pushed it backwards.

Some of the riverbanks were steep. With two small boys as her passengers, Val was driving the truck with a full load up the bank out of the Ord when the front wheels of the truck began to lift off the ground. Thankfully, Val stopped and applied the brakes until I was able to hook on to the front and gently tow the truck forwards and out of danger.

Sean and Daniel were only little tykes but with entirely different perspectives on things. They would often accompany me in the catcher. When we pulled up, I would ask Sean in the passenger seat where home was? Without appearing to even have to think about it, he would always point straight toward the gap in the Hardman Range, even if it wasn't visible. Dan, on the other hand, could always tell where the tucker was!

Turner River Station is, in my eyes, one of the prettiest and most pleasant places I have ever worked on, definitely 'a local phone call to Heaven.' Starting at the Ord River end, it is intersected by the Brooke and Linacre Creeks. Through the boundary gate on the eastern side on to Turner proper, there's the Nicholson River. As one comes through the gap in the Hardman Range, one finds the Turner River. What was called 'the island' was a hunk of country bordered by the Elvira and Panton Rivers, both of which run into the

Chapter 6   Love-a-bull Catchers

They didn't argue with this for long. 1979 Turner River.

Loading the bulls. Turner River.

Bulls caught on The Island, Turner River.

mighty Ord. My personal opinion is that these are Australia's most beautiful rivers. In the distance, 'a little bit long way', to the north, north-west lies the magnificent Osmond Range, Mt Glass and the Bungle Bungles. The sweet red plains of undulations dissected by these rivers was a natural breeding ground for thousands of donkeys, brumbies and, of course, cattle. Little wonder the fragile soil was becoming eroded as the vast tracts of country were unfenced at the time. If one thought for one moment they had an area mustered and cattle all branded, another mob of untouched cattle would emerge from the ranges. The place was like a paradise.

Breakdowns always concerned me so we purchased another short-wheel-base Toyota identical to the catcher and stood it on blocks to provide ready-made spares. However, Kununurra Motors was run by Australia's most proficient spare parts manager. If I contacted Sylvia before midday with an order for spare parts, she could get on to Toyota in Perth and they would have the parts on the 1 pm plane without fail, landing in Kununurra in the evening. We

Goodbye to Turner River and Love-a-bull catchers.

were a mere 320 km from town and 96 km from our nearest neighbour. Our truckie, old Henry, would call by on his way from delivering a load of bulls to Wyndham and we would have the part in hand the following morning. Sadly, that sort of customer service appears to be long gone.

It was with heavy hearts that we returned to the South Burnett as we now had children needing to be schooled and one of my childhood dreams had come to fruition. We purchased 260 hectares of country near Proston and successfully raised stud Limousin cattle there before finally moving to our 111-hectare farm at Tingoora where we currently reside.

And so, from trail rides and picnic lunches (corned beef and damper after ten hours in a saddle) to pitting ourselves against wild bulls in the Kimberly, we consider ourselves to have enjoyed an incredible life that most will only read about, with many amazing people 'cheering us from the stands'. Life is what one makes of it and we will forever be grateful we had the opportunities to stretch ourselves and discover the fortitude that is buried deep within and only needs a bit of tweaking sometimes.

> 'Riches do not consist in the possession of treasures
> but in the use made of them.'
> — Napoleon Bonaparte 1769–1821 Illacius et eatem
> fugiand emporerro core, to eossit, et, sendam nobis
> acipidunt.